Lessons

to

Inspire

Practical Advice from
Successful People

Gary Batara

Addicus Books
Omaha, Nebraska

An Addicus Nonfiction Book

ISBN 978-1-950091-89-8

Cover design by Kit Craven and Jack Kusler
Typography Jack Kusler

Library of Congress Cataloging-in-Publication Data

Names: Batara, Gary, 1982- author.
Title: Lessons to inspire : practical advice from successful people / Gary Batara.
Description: Omaha, Nebraska : Addicus Books, [2024] | Includes bibliographical references.
Identifiers: LCCN 2023056191 | ISBN 9781950091898 (trade paperback) | ISBN 9781950091904 (pdf) | ISBN 9781950091928 (kindle edition) | ISBN 9781950091911 (epub)
Subjects: LCSH: Success in business. | Success. | Conduct of life. | BISAC: SELF-HELP / Self-Management / General | SELF-HELP / Personal Growth / Happiness
Classification: LCC HF5386 .B2726 2024 | DDC 650.1--dc23/eng/20240416
LC record available at https://lccn.loc.gov/2023056191

Addicus Books, Inc.
Omaha, Nebraska 68135
www.AddicusBooks.com
Printed in the United States of America
10 9 8 7 6 5 4 3 2 1

Acknowledgments

First, I wish to acknowledge my loving wife, Marilyn. In the tapestry of my life's journey, you have been the brightest thread, weaving love, support, and unwavering companionship. Your presence is my sanctuary, where ideas flourish and my dreams take flight.

This book is as much yours as it is mine, for it carries the essence of our shared moments—those that challenged me and, in turn, impacted you similarly, and the triumphs of overcoming them hand in hand. This dedication is a humble tribute to the extraordinary woman who is not only my muse but also the beating heart that brings meaning to every word I write. I love you.

I also express my deep appreciation for my family: Didi, Frank, Darren, Val, Dylan, Jake, Radlee, and Alan. There are no words to express my gratitude to each of you.

Introduction

Over a five-year period, I consumed more than 5,000 hours of material from books and online content. I studied personal development, psychology, and philosophy from experts in those fields. Having gleaned this information, I want to share with you the main messages I took away from my reading.

The things I've learned not only helped me turn my life around for the better but helped me achieve goals beyond anything I could ever have imagined. During the twelve months this was written, I became a vice president of a Y-Combinator start-up. I started a marketing consultancy that grew three times, pushing my annual income upward of $450K. I competed in Olympic weightlifting at the national level, placing third in my weight class. I aggressively saved and invested achieving a net worth of $1 million. I completed my master's degree in business administration, with distinction.

Yet these material accomplishments pale in comparison to the journey that led me to be the husband, father, brother, and son I had always aspired to be.

I have drawn on my own experiences from the following quotes, hoping they will resonate with you. It is possible to identify yourself in someone else's story, through a phenomenon known as *neural coupling,* which I discuss in this book. I hope you will discover something meaningful and life-changing within these pages.

1

Progress equals happiness.

—Tony Robbins,
life coach

I have found it highly useful to focus my awareness on moving forward. Making progress—of any kind—is key. Take the case of a $100,000 goal. You can reach that goal by saving a small amount every day. Multiply that amount by the days in a year. However, this plan doesn't always work. Life brings unforeseen challenges that can prevent you from meeting the daily goal.

But if today you save only $1 toward that $100,000, you're still making progress. Maybe not the progress you like, but you have started a habit of saving. The establishment of a regular savings habit gives you the momentum you need to save another dollar, ideally more, the next day.

There's a science to making the journey just as fulfilling as the final outcome. Rewarding yourself for daily progress gives you a mini-dose of dopamine, which creates a lasting reward system for each step toward your goal. Like compound interest, it builds momentum over time. The fulfillment you receive daily builds the confidence you need to achieve what you set out to achieve.

Progress begins with building confidence that you can change. Most people begin with unrealistic expectations, then reinforce their inability to achieve a goal by making the changes too drastic, setting themselves up for failure.

I'm a perfect example of this. I personally hated the journey, with a passion. Instead of offering me daily rewards, it fueled my self-anger. I had condemned myself to this impossible task, and would never tell anyone that I was only hoping things would work out.

It is actually extremely rare to stumble upon success. I didn't know which was worse: feeling disappointment that I'd set myself up for being unable to achieve something, merely by writing it down, or feeling disappointment for not even writing it down. For years, I never developed goals, because where I was was often so far from where I wanted to be.

Actor Will Smith once told a story about building a brick wall. As a kid, it seemed like an impossible task. His father taught him that it isn't about how impossible a task might seem, take the time to lay one brick, just one, as perfectly as a brick can be laid.

Stop pressuring yourself to achieve your goals tomorrow. Small, daily progress is an often-overlooked achievement. The compounding of daily progress can offer a greater sense of accomplishment than the attainment of the goal.

2

*The value is not in accomplishing a goal, but
what achieving a goal will make of you.*

—Jim Rohn,
American entrepreneur, writer

I was taught to set goals and hold myself accountable. If I did that, then on the day I suddenly achieved a specific goal, I would feel a sense of accomplishment. As a husband and father of two—nearly a decade after all my friends had already graduated—I went back to school to get my undergraduate degree, believing I would finally achieve my goal and be fulfilled.

After graduation, however, I felt empty. The weekends were no longer spent waking up at 3 A.M. to study before my kids terrorized the house, or hitting the books late at night, only to fall asleep in an empty Starbucks. Not only did I no longer have something to work toward, I no longer had that daily push to think differently.

Still, my education helped me realize that completing an assignment, organizing a group project, or completing an online exam—on time—was simply part of the journey. Some days I enjoy what I have to do, and other days, not so much. In the end, working as hard as I can each day, then doing it again the next day, knowing I wouldn't see immediate results, changed something inside me, for the better. In my experience, this practice is particularly useful when trying something physically challenging, such as running a marathon, losing weight, taking on a daily steps challenge, or really any challenge you doubt your body is capable of.

You build a mind-body connection through consistent daily effort. This enables you to enhance your capabilities. It bolsters your confidence to stretch mentally and succeed.

Similar principles can be applied to physical accomplishments. Why lose weight? Why run a marathon? Sometimes training gets monotonous, and you wonder why the hell you're in a gym at 6 A.M., or are eating a salad instead of a burger on a Saturday night. When you're in the thick of it, that grind gives you a sense of meaning, of purpose, and of confidence that goes beyond immediate gratification. Strenuous work strips away the surface-level satisfaction and exposes what really drives you, revealing your "why."

In fact, this gift is applicable to all areas of your life and to every challenge you face. Through achieving a goal, you completely rewire your brain, getting comfortable with discomfort. When you do what you need to do to accomplish a goal, it expands your mindset. This has a direct impact on how you approach other challenges in your life. The best part about this is that you will have experienced success and won long before you achieve your goal.

3

Sometimes you're the problem.

—Simon Sinek,
writer, speaker

I used to blame everyone and everything around me when I wasn't getting what I wanted. At one time, I nearly lost my marriage, friends, and family due to this debilitating mindset. I built up resentment toward so many people, because I thought people should change so I could get what I wanted in life. I needed career growth. Those in power needed to give me an opportunity.

I did it with my friends. If only they would keep me in the loop and invite me out more, there would be no drama. I did it with my family. If only they saw things my way, then we'd be closer. I did it with my wife. If she could just be happy all the time, I would be happy as well. I did it with my kids. If only they would cry less and be less needy, then I would have more time to do what I want. Even my dog would have been more enjoyable if she didn't need to go to the bathroom so often.

It's a poisonous mentality that compounds over time and makes you blind to your own victimization. This behavior leads to isolation, depression, and anger. You can't control what happens around you, but you can control your reaction to it.

There's an adage, that life is 10 percent what happens to you and 90 percent what you do about it. In Canadian

5

psychologist and writer Jordan Peterson's words: don't be afraid of snakes in the garden, or attempt to avoid them. Instead, get yourself a sword so you can chop them up into small pieces.

You will almost certainly face challenges in this world, so arm yourself with the realization that you are the only thing you can control in this world. The insight that you're the source of your own happiness, and sadness, is very empowering.

True accountability is a scary notion. Take a look inside, and really ask yourself, "what completely dumb things am I doing right now?" To see yourself staring right back into your own eyes is kind of a bummer, but the beauty of that exact moment is, once you see you're your own problem, you're also staring right at your solution.

4

*You never know when someone needs you
to be at your best.*

—Les Brown, former
Ohio State Representative

When my wife and I were having the hardest time in our marriage, I knew I was being a terrible husband. I kept asking myself, "why can't I just do what I know I should do to improve our marriage?" I wallowed in self-loathing, depression, and self-pity that I seemed to be incapable of changing.

Then one day I found myself giving advice on lifting technique to a stranger at the gym. It was a small gesture, but that day I happened to notice it was making me feel amazing, a feeling that persisted throughout the day. It reminded me of the great feelings I used to have when I was being a great husband.

It was a big moment of clarity around perception. Although I felt totally useless in one area of my life, when I was dealing with a stranger in a completely different area, my value felt enormous.

During this time, I befriended people at the gym and became the "advice guy." At that time, I also saw my interactions with my wife improve. Using the gym as my venue, I was developing the skills of mindful listening and empathy. After a few months, I found people were approaching me, hoping for some positive change. They had seen those changes in others at the gym, and knew

7

I'd been spending time with them. They asked me, how did I know so many people? How did I know so much about lifting? What exactly was I saying that made people seem so engaged at 5 in the morning?

People sought me out asking for advice about depression, anxiety, confidence issues, relationships, even career guidance. Over the course of a year, I made a significant impact on twelve individuals. Each became a daily reminder, to be my best self at the gym, even amid my own problems. The benefits were useful not only to me, but to those around me.

I was healing myself, as well as my marriage, by helping others solve their problems instead of focusing on mine.

Never underestimate the value that you bring to the world just by being your best self on a daily basis. There's likely someone out there counting on you to be just that.

5

Decide what kind of life you actually want, then say no to everything else that isn't that.

—James and Claudia Altucher,
The Power of No

Saying no is stigmatized. Connotations associated with the word no suggest that you will hurt someone's feelings, because they likely expected a yes. Saying no may lead you to feel guilt or fear. Some believe if others say no, they'll be unable to take advantage of opportunities.

In my experience, saying yes all the time disguises a need for acceptance. When an intimate relationship begins, you'll find it easy to say yes more often, As a way of demonstrating how much you care for another person. Saying yes implies you're both on the same page. You affirm each other.

All this logic seemed to make sense, until I became a father. Then saying yes became a thing of the past. Saying no became the norm, because I knew it was for the benefit of my children. The power of no became a great reminder: not always saying yes actually has benefit. Yes meant we were in love. It meant we were on the same page; we were aligned.

At the time, I didn't know that saying yes was my way of gaining silent acceptance from someone. I didn't realize how much this could hurt me. As a result, I was too frequently saying no to my own needs.

Money and material things come and go, but time and energy are precious commodities we can never get back. To say no is to create the life you want. Cut out the things that, deep down, you know don't serve you. Say a resounding yes to yourself, to the things you find most important, that give you meaning and fulfillment in your own life. Double down on things that bring you fulfillment, and cut those that drain you.

For me today, saying no still requires mindfulness as an ongoing process. But it has helped me identify my self-destructive behavior patterns. Two things I always have to remind myself: first, saying no is okay, and secondly, don't always say no to yourself.

6

*Your need for acceptance can
make you invisible in this world.*

—Jim Carrey,
actor, comedian

I was blown away by this statement by Jim Carrey. As a funny kid, I learned early to use humor to get attention, acceptance, and validation. I studied people who were funny or popular, and practiced their speech patterns, mannerisms, and style. Surely, I thought, that would be the ticket, to replicate someone else's personality and claim it as my own. Unfortunately, I was able to do just that. My childhood bullies were distracted by my humor. Instead of being picked on, I was welcomed into the lives of people I was never meant to be close to.

Throughout school, I was the life of the party, always entertaining others with jokes. Popularity, girls, and praise followed. I hid my real self, wearing a mask, and it seemed to bring success. All along, it was having a negative effect on me.

It was easy to believe the world knew me for what I was, but there was something gnawing at me that I couldn't ignore. The more acceptance I received, the less I liked myself. I was always in need of new material, new jokes. It was never enough. I had to be always funnier and to do more and more outrageous things to maintain the approval of my peers. By the time I started college, I didn't know who I really was.

The desire for acceptance was no longer there. In an environment with thousands of other kids, I felt faceless. At eighteen, I asked myself for the first time, what would people think if I did what I wanted rather than what they expect of me? Could I handle it? I started to notice that when I did what I want, even if it didn't make me popular, I felt a greater self-confidence than what I could gain from wowing the crowd.

I found that building self-confidence is only as strong as the foundation you lay it on. I stopped seeking acceptance, and welcomed any stares or disdain people have. Part of why it's hard for people to see you change is because you fit a part in their life as you were. When you change, it has a direct impact on them, a ripple effect you cannot hide from. I lost friends; it didn't take long for hundreds to drop to just a few.

Nearly twenty years later, those few are closer to me than ever, but the self-confidence I built by displaying my true identity is priceless.

7

Don't cry because it's over;
smile because it happened.

—Brendon Burchard,
High Performance Habits

We often hear that people come and go in our lives, some for a reason, some for a season, some for a lifetime. Those who come for a reason are there to teach you something or to offer you a unique experience. People who come in a season offer that experience, gift, or lesson over a specific period of time. Those you cherish for a lifetime are your gift, a blessing that remains by your side even when season and reason pass.

Throughout my life, the more people I came in contact with, the more I found their perspective on life to be different from mine. These were the people who made the most lasting impressions and offered the most invaluable lessons.

There are times in your life when you meet people you've feel you've been waiting for your whole life. People who say things you've only thought about saying. People who have done things you've always wanted to do. Intimate relationships, or family, friends, coworkers, even strangers. That they are potentially anywhere makes them more precious, because you will never know if one of these valuable interactions is taking place at the moment.

In the past, I would compare myself to yesterday, wondering if the person I was during that interaction would last. Could I move forward without them? Yet to do so would totally negate the value of that experience.

I've found that whenever you have grieved the loss of someone, a part of the healing process is living purposefully and paying homage to those experiences by fully living their lessons. Don't let that precious moment in time be wasted, allowing yourself to slip back to being the person you were before you met the one you now grieve. In my experience, to move forward, be present and to honor the richness of an experience by not wasting it is a driving force.

Romanticizing the past only lures you back there, when in fact its impermanence is what makes it so special. Embrace the fact that cherished interactions are endless wells from which you can draw strength in the present. You don't know if or when you'll see that person again, but if you do, you'll be able to live up to the lessons they taught. This becomes a reciprocal gift, a subtle reminder: who you are today is a direct reflection of your time spent together.

8

*We all know what to do, but none of us know
how to make ourselves do it.*

—Mel Robbins,
5 Second Rule

Mel Robbins developed a five-second rule. The idea is to count down from five. When you reach one, you act. Immediately.

Those of you who have heard of Robbins have probably learned how she turned her life around by identifying those micro-moments in life where she was faced with a choice. If we can capture those moments, before our brains interfere and we're overwhelmed by our inner critics, we can trick both mind and body into action despite our traditional and often limiting behaviors.

Learning this persuaded me to look at every moment in my life, every day. On any given day, there are hundreds or thousands of moments when I know I should be doing something, but I don't. As I let time pass, I tell myself maybe next time, I'll react differently.

Everybody identifies these moments in their own way. Maybe it's reaching out to a loved one, speaking up in a meeting, or standing up to someone who is bullying. We have all faced moments where we're just one decision away from leading an entirely different life. If you're anything like me, you feel disgusted with yourself when you do nothing. But simply being able to recognize these moments has lasting value. This principle still works for

15

me when I find myself continuing a negative behavior, whether in an intimate relationship, career, or friendships.

The ability to recognize where I could have made a better choice has helped me prevent that negative behavior from gaining momentum. I experience moments that cause me anxiety, the anxiety of failing, the anxiety of being ridiculed, or my own self-doubt. I will count down from five and act anyway.

When I've done this, it hasn't had a happy ending. Actually, the opposite. Taking action usually results in failure, but over time, I've developed a sense of satisfaction from taking action. A lasting positive impact on my life has come from taking action despite reservations. For me, the five-second rule has been the key to opening possibilities.

In the same way, dealing with the repercussions I've incurred as a result of my decision has been an immensely rewarding journey. I've found that no matter what, I will always be able to take action. With continuous action, confidence grows. A rewiring of how you approach life occurs, and recognizing where you must stop is a terrifying but fulfilling avenue for change.

9

*The best way to find yourself is
to lose yourself in the service of others.*

—Mahatma Gandhi,
world leader, political activist

After nearly a decade as a husband, I understand the value of this quote. I was so excited to become a husband. To have someone to love every day, someone to do kind things for, someone to inspire me to become my highest self. I had publicly pledged to hold myself accountable to the promises I made to my wife, her family, my family, and our loved ones.

I didn't know this at the time, but now I'm so glad that's how it began. I was fortunate to not enter the relationship with the purpose of getting something out of it. Rather I entered with the purpose of giving. It was a world where doing good and being kind are rewarded.

The most difficult years of my relationship with my wife were those in which I had lost sight of this. As a result, I withdrew and took from the relationship instead of giving to it. The relationship became like a diminished bank account. At some point there weren't any funds left. I was overdrawn.

Searching for fulfillment elsewhere, I began to take from others, in various areas of my life. There was a possibility of that happening with friends, family, or colleagues. Whatever I could get out of them was the thing that mattered.

17

The idea of rock bottom has always seemed like living in a cold apartment, in the inner city, with no food on the table. The exact opposite was true. I just saw how much people were willing to give and I took advantage of it.

When I changed my mindset, my career took off. I began to draw notice from women. At that time, I was probably as far as I had ever been from being great husband material. My personal kingdom was built on the kindness and generosity of those who cared for me. My worst self was on full display and I was at my lowest. I had to achieve my own egocentric aims before I realized how unhealthy my lifestyle was, as well as the effect it had on those around me.

I began to thirst again for meaning in my life, apart from self-interest. I went back to the source and started by doing small, kind things for my wife. I wanted to be the person I knew I could be. Through this new perspective, being a great husband transitioned to being a better father, brother, and son. Today I see in the mirror a man I do not shy away from.

My journey to redemption was fueled by the outward focus of finding ways to offer value to those I loved and adored, to benefit those around me.

I've seen what selfishness breeds. It breeds more selfishness. Taking care of others and serving a purpose greater than one's own is the path to becoming your best self. In order to become selfless, I had first to be completely selfish.

10

Join the 5 A.M. club.

—Robin Sharma,
The 5 A.M. Club

I've always gotten up early and consider myself a morning person. I used to wake up early in order to watch cartoons. Most days, I watched infomercials, as it was so early in the morning.

When I became an adult, my morning persona was challenged when I joined a 5 A.M. CrossFit class. After a few months, I noticed something. I started going to bed earlier, in order to have more energy and keep up with the athletes in the class. Then, I began to prepare my clothes and pack my lunch for the next day. As a result, I ate differently, because I didn't want to feel sluggish during the class. I even studied the movements the night before.

Unintentionally, I discovered a discipline I didn't know I lacked. The small details necessary to perform at my best required these preceding steps.

Having found that mindset, I tried to do more tasks in advance, making it likelier I was prepared for success. The practice of waking up early enabled me to discover what I could do to improve my entire day and, ultimately, my life.

To extend that mindset, I began doing dishes after eating rather than waiting until they piled up. I made lunches for my wife and kids to save their time, a small but positive start to their day.

Being up early every day gave me time to ponder. Every time I woke up early, I realized what I could do with the two hours that I would have spent sleeping. The things you like to do when no one else is awake will surprise you. It's sort of like recess, but for adults. I've found that early rising motivates me to be better. Moreover, early rising benefits those around you. At a time when the rest of the world wakes, you already have the day's plan in mind. This results in more time for being of service to others.

Imagine the times when you'd have helped someone, but you were in a hurry, running behind. Every such situation was a missed opportunity to be of assistance to someone.

The impact of each act of assistance is incalculable. There is no shortage of time, but a surplus. When you use the early morning hours to prepare for your day, you're developing the discipline to become the best version of yourself, benefiting everyone around you.

11

*We cannot think of being acceptable to others
until we have first proven acceptable to ourselves.*

—Malcolm X,
human rights activist

Growing up, self-acceptance was a problem for me. As a child, I was smaller than most kids, slightly awkward, and had a slight stutter, which I found embarrassing. Added to this, I was the youngest of three, making growing up more challenging.

As a result, I sought acceptance early, in order to avoid being excluded or even bullied by my peers. I gradually realized that my ability to make people laugh could be my pathway to acceptance. I became popular. I was able to bring joy and lighten the mood in any situation, even in large crowds—the entire school kind of crowd.

It was the acceptance of others that allowed me to accept myself, or at least accept the person I considered myself to be. From grade school to high school, humor was my persona.

Being humorous was my mask. I was playing a character. However, there was a drawback. I discovered that if you let others define you, you won't discover your true self. Worse for me, I was being praised for being funny. Even though I worked well with crowds, I was also uncomfortable due to my choice to play the humorous character.

Jay Shetty, a British influencer, once said, "I am not what I think I am; I am not what you think I am; I am what I think you think I am..." This is a frightening idea, that someone else's idea of who you are can become your own. Self-acceptance involves being okay with who you are and what brings you joy, regardless of how others may feel. It's easy to believe you have one unique characteristic that defines you. It never occurred to me that I could be a summation of many attributes, a melting pot of characteristics that truly shaped who I was. You can be who you choose to be, whether you're extroverted or introverted. Accepting that you can be who you are is a beautiful moment of clarity.

As a funny guy, I've learned you can connect with people from all walks of life. However, the key is authenticity. Observing the crowds' acceptance made me realize that people recognize and appreciate a vulnerable person who can make them laugh. When I saw joy on their faces, I yearned to feel the same. Humor became my path to self-acceptance. I became an excellent public speaker, but I wouldn't have that ability if I hadn't questioned the very acceptance I was so eager to obtain.

12

*The effect you have on others
is the most valuable currency there is.*

—Jim Carrey,
actor, comedian

Have you ever wondered why you may find yourself reminiscing about someone from your past, someone you have not spoken to recently? This happens to me often. When I think of the time I spent with that person, it brings a smile to my face and warms my heart. There is a saying that you rarely remember the words or the specifics of an interaction with someone, but you will never forget how the person made you feel. Through the years, I have accumulated laughs, tears, smiles, and victories that have been fundamental to my self-esteem. I didn't realize nostalgia for someone I once knew allowed me to do just that.

Nostalgia serves a positive function, inspiring us to remember the past in our lives. It allows us to recall our authentic self and compare that with who we are now. In this way, we see who we want to be in the future. Nostalgia helps us strengthen our sense of self, our identity.

I sometimes wonder about the times certain people in my life had a deep impact on me. I wonder whether I am a person who others remember. To me, this is a romantic notion, knowing that I can, at any given moment, be giving someone a lasting memory that could change their life forever. This has helped me stay focused and be aware of my interactions. It gives me a positive outlook on life, knowing that my value to the world and those around me cannot be underestimated.

As I think about all that has taken place in my life, this treasure chest full of priceless moments, it triggers me to wonder who I would be today if I were to pass that on to someone else. In a similar way, I also reflect on all the "bad" I've put into this world and the countless interactions where I chose to tear down and belittle. These moments, too, have lasting effects on others. As I think about my guilt and shame over such moments, it has led me to want to be a better person. It seems to me that putting good into the world is one of our most important social responsibilities. To this day, I treasure my past wonderful fond memories as a guide for how to conduct myself in this life, offering what I've been fortunate enough to receive, as well as giving back to others who have given to me.

13

*Make friends with people
who want the best for you.*

—Jordan Peterson,
psychologist

As a well-liked kid, I thought everyone was my friend. By my definition, friends are here to make our lives better. In my ignorance, I didn't know the difference between someone who helps you to improve and someone who lets you become stagnant. There's guilt associated with judging between the two. It may seem a selfish notion, to judge people and cut them out of your life. I can attest that you can have dozens, maybe even hundreds of people around you, but still feel completely alone and unknown.

As Jordan Peterson points out, we each have to surround ourselves with people who want to see us grow. This is a social responsibility, an unspoken contract we have with one another. You want people around you to hold you to a high standard. That's not always fun, but you want people to hold you accountable for doing things that can hurt you.

Understanding this concept was quite difficult for a long time. I'd always assumed that my hundreds of friends each fit into an essential category of people I needed in my life. These categories included athletics, partiers, co-workers, my church group, grade school, high school, and college friends. Deciding which friendships were important to me involved guilt. Who am I to say whether an individual is worthwhile?

Then one day, I realized I couldn't judge a friend's value to me unless I took a closer look at myself. I'd ask myself whether I was offering value to them. Was I interacting with them more than just on weekends? What did I know about them, or worse, did I even care to know them? It became clear to me that I myself didn't offer much value to some of them.

I decided to simply stop interacting with these people. In my mind, I was saving them from an unproductive friendship. I needed to end these superficial friendships. I believed there would be more room for others, to whom I would be able to devote more time and make them closer friends.

I believed I'd never contact these people again, but in fact I did make an effort to reach out to them. I called them, thanking them for our time spent together. I acknowledged that our journey had been extremely meaningful to me, that I would never forget them. In honor of those friendships, I resolved to never forget the lessons we learned together, and to use their memories as foundational bricks for everything that followed.

I am to this day grateful for those who crossed my path. I did my best to keep in touch with those who appreciated the value I offered them. I still do everything I can to keep in touch with the few friends I keep by my side today.

Don't surround yourself only with those who help you grow. Decide whether you're willing to invest time and energy into their growth. If the answer is no, take responsibility and don't waste their time.

14

Discipline equals freedom.

—Jocko Willink,
retired officer, United States Navy

I was forever changed by this quote. How could it be possible? As a child, I associated discipline, with a negative connotation, as a consequence of having done something wrong. Today, I have come to think of discipline as the highest form of self-care.

At first, discipline sounded limiting. During my day, I'd wander aimlessly about, fingers crossed, hoping it would be a good day, that I'd feel content. I didn't consider the creation of a structure to arrange to have the day I really wanted.

That was my starting point. When I got up, I started taking a few minutes to plan out my day. I'd use that plan to highlight all the things that I didn't want to do. In turn, this helped me highlight the things I actually enjoyed and wanted to do more of.

Over time, I became better at looking beyond an individual day, to a week, a month, and finally an entire year. To maximize my fun time, I scheduled the things I was not necessarily looking forward to in such a way that I could devote more time to things I would enjoy. The realization that I could create my own happiness by scheduling the things that brought me fulfillment was an amazing moment of clarity for me. The Willink quote has come to mean a lot to me. I've adopted the idea that discipline equals freedom—freedom to do more of what makes you happy.

Taking care of the things I didn't feel like doing was simply something I looked forward to, because it got me closer to doing the things I really wanted to do. I gained an enormous amount of self-confidence. This helped me in other aspects of my life. The accomplishment of things that didn't seem fun became just as rewarding as doing the fun things. Over the years, I've been able to accomplish things I once believed impossible.

Having realized how discipline is the highest form of self-care, ensuring that I can depend on myself to do the difficult things, I appreciate its significance even more. Discipline, which I'd thought to be a negative word, turned out to be a remedy for my shortcomings.

Cultivating discipline is a lifestyle change that enables one to delay immediate gratification in exchange for sustained joy and fulfillment in the long run. I now look forward to the reward on the other end. The discipline that Jocko referenced has taught me that yes, it offers freedom and self-care. My greatest lesson from this is, discipline became an avenue that enabled me to overcome self-doubt.

15

What makes you vulnerable
makes you beautiful.

—Brené Brown,
The Power of Vulnerability

I spent years learning self-acceptance. Learning shared values from my family and friends, I created a path to constant rewards for certain behaviors. These behaviors included obeying the rules of my parents and my siblings and playing the role of entertainer for my friends. Although it appeared as if playing by the rules of others had rewards, I wasn't really doing what I wanted to do, so those rewards were meaningless.

In her book *The Four Agreements,* author Don Miguel Ruiz discusses the rules we learn as children. Later, as adults, we unknowingly continue to abide by them. For me, it was a form of domestication. I no longer needed to be taught or have rules imposed upon me; I simply absorbed them into every part of my being. I embodied the traits that earned me rewards and became extremely proficient at exercising them. I very rarely got into trouble, or maybe "caught" is the better word.

I could sense what people needed from me and would proactively provide it. In effect, it was like a job. Although I never really felt I was being my authentic self, I had an excellent map to the precise activities that result in a very specific social reward.

I discovered the same thing in relationships. I've been married for more than ten years and have seen how bad behavior can damage a relationship.

Almost robotically, I did and said the things that I believed my wife expected of me. I did this so much that there were years during which I don't even remember arguing. I waited years before I finally asked her what she wanted from me, what she wanted from a husband. Her response was, "Just be yourself." But in my mind, if I were truly myself, I would make mistakes, I would be selfish, and I would do things that weren't what stereotypical good husbands and fathers are expected to do. If I were imperfect, she wouldn't love me.

The truth is, I was afraid to be vulnerable with her. Strangely enough, it was easier to be vulnerable with a complete stranger. As I started to create connections with complete strangers, I reminded myself this person doesn't really know me. What am I losing if I share all my deepest, darkest fears with them? In this environment of zero judgment, I learned that being vulnerable can be a powerful magic mirror or a reset button, that allows me to see my true self.

At first, it was frightening to express my inner thoughts out loud. Over time I learned it's an incredible gift to share vulnerability with the people closest to me, allowing them to see the real me, imperfections and all. When we do and say things just to gain approval from others, we create distance between ourselves and others. By doing it, you inadvertently isolate yourself. The most significant thing I learned during this time was that there's a universal desire to know we're not alone. Being vulnerable fosters deeper connections and a sense of community with those around you.

Being true to myself has opened the door to the deepest connections and fulfillment I have ever experienced, whereas doing all the right things can never satisfy.

16

Fear kills growth.

—Gary Vaynerchuck,
entrepreneur

I consider myself to be fairly fearless. In my early search for acceptance, I found that doing things no one else was willing to do gave me a level of self-confidence that positively impacted other aspects of my life. My bravery didn't come from doing these things, but by attempting them, I opened the door to my own growth.

My willingness to do anything allowed me to gain acceptance and distract people from my inadequacies. By doing and saying crazy things, I gave the impression I was fearless. As an adult looking back, I know there were countless times I likely should have been dead. No, seriously. From spinning out at seventy-five miles per hour on a highway for a laugh, to the countless times I've broken bones and required stitches after wowing the crowd, I courted disaster.

Being an entertainer was also a useful skill when I entered the workforce. Though I wasn't looking to gain laughs or acceptance, I was still trying to set myself apart from the crowd.

There is a do-or-die thing that happens when you're on a public stage and you have a 100 percent chance of failing. It elicits a flight or fight response. In my experi-

31

ence, I discovered I was likely to choose fight. It wasn't a matter of being brave; it was about knowing that if I put myself in a situation where I couldn't get away, I could still rely on myself to make it through.

There's a saying, "you must burn your boats in order to take the island." You're not aware of your inner strength until you face consequences on stage, and fail. Even if you just want to avoid looking stupid, the fact that you put yourself out there has lasting value. Each time you do it, you learn you can do the scary things in life. You'll also find that more of these opportunities will present themselves to you.

For example, you might raise your hand in a meeting, ask someone out on a date, or even speak out when you feel it's necessary. Rather than asking yourself what you have to lose, start by asking yourself what you have to gain. For me, this benefit-based decision-making process makes it easier to go after something and stay focused on the reward. Take fear as an instrument you can use to set the stage for achieving your goals. You will be surprised by your ability to deliver.

17

It doesn't matter whose fault it is.
Fault and responsibility do not go together.

—Will Smith,
American actor

My life was changed by this idea. When I first heard this quote, I actually got upset. I was so stuck on right versus wrong. I believed that anyone who had done wrong absolutely needed to be held accountable for it. If a person sincerely regretted what they did, it's their responsibility to make amends. In my experience, that happening is more the exception than the rule. My life has been filled with people that I left behind, because I didn't think they ever really understood just how hurtful they were to me. I harbored years of resentment.

In the end, all this led to was the degradation of my character. The feelings of hurt I had harbored instilled a habit of criticizing those close to me. As someone who has battled passive-aggressive issues for years, this was like a drug. My addiction was dwelling on victimhood, finding ways people hurt me, and telling myself that any forward progress is halted until they make things right.

The problem with that philosophy is that my happiness becomes contingent on the actions of others. If this is the kind of thing you do, it's most likely you're the one with the problem. You're stuck in the past, and probably depending on someone else to fix things.

Likely, it will never happen. When you hold onto past hurts, you're taking poison and hoping its effects will be felt by the one who hurt you.

There is freedom in letting go of what has happened; letting go of assigning to others the responsibility to make things right in your life. Free yourself from the bonds of the past. This is not saying that a wrong done to you was okay. Rather you simply acknowledge it happened.

I had to ask myself what I would do about the things that hurt me. My well-being was at risk. I was the one sitting with the hurt, and no one was coming to save me.

In such a situation, it is likely that someone does deserve an apology, but waiting for one just wastes time and energy. Move instead toward something more productive. The anger and hurt may never be completely gone, but we all deserve to move forward. Release yourself from this broken mentality. If you really want to find what you're looking for, rely on your own actions and not those of another.

18

Greatness pulls mediocrity into the mud.

—David Goggins,
retired United States Navy SEAL

If you're anything like me, you enjoy watching people do amazing things. For me, nothing is more inspirational than watching someone accomplish something that seems impossible. There is also nothing more uncomfortable, in a less-inspiring way, than witnessing something like this in real life. When I started to watch people actually do amazing things in real life, I felt very uncomfortable with myself and could not understand why. It was a mirror I didn't want to look into. I would tell myself, this person was probably born athletic, has genes that make them smart; they have a gift.

It was easier for me to comprehend another's accomplishments when it was, because they have innate talent rather than that they succeeded by hard work. It seemed strange to me that someone could work hard at something with no apparent end in sight. Just to work hard for the sake of doing their best. I witnessed amazing things that peers did in grade school and high school, but I told myself their abilities weren't meant for me. Such a mentality would ultimately move me away from accomplishing my goals. However, working hard for its own sake is the fire you need to embark on a personal journey in the first place.

Still, the idea of achieving greatness scared me. It seemed like a daunting task. Why not just have fun and relax? Our lives are often guided by our fears, disguised as practicality.

As the comedian Jim Carrey once said, I lived that way for many years until I discovered cooking. It was through cooking that I became aware of just how lazy I had been.

For minimum wage, many people work like their lives are on the line. For most people working in kitchens, the fear is often real. Losing their job means losing their livelihood.

I had this experience. Once, my dream was to become an executive chef. I started as a dishwasher, then as a cook. I was very committed to my work, but I hadn't even a fraction of the work ethic or knowledge required. For me, it was all about titles, salaries, and selfish ambition. Daily, I would observe these people, making sure their preparation was perfect, making sure the kitchen ran smoothly. These chefs' primary motivation was just to make their dishes the best they could possibly be. It was their pride and full ownership of their craft.

In addition, chefs are on their feet for 12 to 14 hours a day, 10 to 14 days in a row. They often work double shifts. They also had lives outside the kitchen. They were fathers and husbands, mothers, and wives. It was a lifestyle, a culture, to which they dedicate themselves. They put in hard work daily, perfecting their craft. It gave them a sense of pride and it was an expression of their identity.

From more than a decade in the kitchen I learned that no matter what your endeavor is, you must give everything you have to it, not for the reward, but rather for the fulfillment that comes from applying your full focus. The noblest thing in life is doing hard things when no one notices, knowing it won't lead to fame or fortune.

19

*Not until we are lost
do we begin to understand ourselves.*

—Henry David Thoreau,
Walden

Admitting I am lost was a form of failure to me. I felt I always had to check all the boxes, do all the things I saw other people doing. My childhood was filled with advice and hoary scripts about getting an education, getting a good job, getting married, buying a house, and having children. I accomplished these things early in life. A pragmatic approach to life worked great until I got to the part in the story that no one discusses; the part after the movie ends. Okay, so I'm a thirty-two-year-old guy with a family. Now, what?

I couldn't see the beauty of what I had. I kept looking to the horizon to see what was coming next. I would have the rest of my life to enjoy my amazing wife, family, and home, though I couldn't see it at the time. As a result of becoming a father and family man, my life had changed. All I could see, though, was what I'd no longer be able to do. The quick fun vacations with my wife were now shadowed by all the things we couldn't do. We had a newborn child. We had diaper bags, bottles, clothes, and milk that needed to be packed. The experience of trying out a new restaurant or attending movies was no longer easy to do. At work, extra projects that would have expanded my career were put on hold so I'd be more available to help with the baby.

At that time, I had no perspective of what I'd gained. I viewed the world through the lens of what I'd lost. I thought I was a bad father, and I was. As dramatic as it sounds, I felt I was experiencing symptoms over the life I had lost, as if I were an addict going through withdrawal. Agonizing over the past, I read books and blogs about how some people are just not built for parenthood, and there is nothing one can do about it. I was trying to figure out how to get out of this. I had an excuse to be a victim. I'd reached rock bottom at a time when many other men were finding purpose in their lives. My identity—or rather my ego—was shaken to the core. Being ungrateful was my biggest failure.

As the saying goes, when you're at rock bottom, you can only go up. The shallowness of my own selfish desires became apparent to me. I did not like the person I saw. I told myself enough was enough, that I hated being this selfish and ungrateful. I would never get back the early years in my children's lives. That realization brought me to tears. In order to grow, I had to let go of so many things that had led me to this point. I had to become a new person, and this time I wasn't going to follow the prescribed path.

With this breakdown, I experienced something amazing. My once-cherished feelings of purpose, excitement, and promise flooded back into my life. It was as if I was growing up at the same time as my children.

There is something sentimental about letting go of the old me and leaning into a new perspective. There's actually a beauty in having your world turned upside down. It causes you to embrace change and advance down an unpaved road, leading you to the birth of a new perspective that would otherwise never have been discovered.

20

*He who has a why to live
can bear almost any how.*

—Freidrich Nietzche,
philosopher

An idea I heard once struck me; it was that motivation is garbage. For most of my life, I lived on motivation. I believed that my life always moved forward when motivation, like a mystical force, moved me to action. Most days, I waited for motivation to strike. As I got older, I realized that motivation is not garbage, but instead should be the driving force behind your actions. Your purpose will always be your true call to action, however. It is actually the creator of those moments of motivation. The purpose is a guiding light. It will remind you why you're on the path you're on.

I came across something American entrepreneur Tom Bilyeu once said. It provided a logic that helped me clarify the path I'm on. Bilyeu said it was his purpose in life to acquire as many utilitarian skills as possible and to use them for something greater than himself.

This concept helps me cope with days when I want to be lazy and selfish. Each time I think about the things I don't want to do I also think about how my life won't get better as a result of an inability to motivate myself. Being aware that I'm part of a greater network of people that count on me to perform my best. This realization helped me change my perspective of what to do when life gets tough, as it eventually always does.

Purpose isn't just an umbrella on a rainy day. It's a reminder that rain brings new life. As I began to perceive my life's purpose through this lens, I discovered a strength and resilience during adversity. I realized I could apply this to all of my challenges. As I approach different stages in life, I develop something to pull me forward. As I live my purpose each day, it gradually becomes clearer to me. After having children, that purpose became more evident. I was reminded how responsible I am for those around me. Even on my worst days, I can still be of value to people.

The younger version of me would have run from that kind of responsibility. I stumbled upon the gift of purpose, because of my inadequacy.

I grew up surrounded by material abundance. I thought life was an endless orchard of fruit. As I grew older, I realized the only reason there is shade today is because someone planted a tree decades ago. We each possess a unique purpose in life, and each purpose is a superpower that allows us to lift ourselves up. Motivation relies on energy to fuel short-term bursts of action and achieve satisfaction, but it doesn't lead to a deeper drive and fulfillment. Those can be found only by discovering your purpose.

21

How you choose to be treated is on you.

—Lisa Nichols,
motivational speaker

In her story, Lisa Nichols recounts to us her father's view of how a woman should be treated when she's on a date. He taught her an important lesson: at the end of the night, how she chooses to be treated is up to her.

Growing up, I just assumed some people would treat me well and others wouldn't. I never considered each interaction was driven by a choice I had made. I would leave it up to chance, hoping people would treat me as kindly and warmly as I treated them. I was not taught to stand up and speak up for myself. Many of us spend a great deal of our lives accepting hurtful behaviors from others, because we think that's just the way people are. It's a highly restrictive and debilitating mindset.

Interrupting the normal flow of interactions was like jumping off the deep end for the first time. I knew I'd survive, but still, it was terrifying to consider just how much unpleasantness I was about to experience. I've experienced hundreds of instances when I knew I should have been better treated. I kept my mouth shut, hoping to avoid conflict. In spite of the rewards gained when I allowed others to treat me poorly, the effort required to confront conflict discouraged me. I now had no idea how well I could face conflict. Instead, I avoided it. I told

41

myself being agreeable was a form of kindness. But being agreeable to avoid conflict resulted in dishonest harmony. What I needed was honest harmony.

I realized I couldn't continue overlooking the effect of my choices about how I was treated. There was always a direct correlation between my response to ill treatment and the effects that followed. If I allowed myself to be treated poorly, I'd be given less important tasks. I wouldn't be included in important meetings. I'd be overlooked for promotions and salary increases. If I allow the bad behavior of others to stand, it becomes a pattern of that person's behavior.

Dishonest harmony breeds passive-aggressive behavior, behavior that in the long run is toxic. I started taking baby steps, speaking up when something didn't sit well with me. At first, when I spoke up during a conflict, I would stutter, my heart would race, and my hands would shake. But I was on the way up. I knew things couldn't get any worse, so dealing with conflict became easier. If I could understand my reaction, I could prepare myself for the next time.

In defense of those who might be harming you, keep an open mind. Many people do respond positively to an opportunity for change. The majority of the time when I took the chance, I found they were willing to both listen and to adapt their behavior. In any case, you'll benefit whether they change or not. Keep in mind how you want to be treated and avoid silence in the face of disrespect. This will raise your self-confidence, and as a bonus, give you a definitive answer about this person's place in your life. Each time you practice this constructive behavior, you get better at it. It doesn't make life perfect, but it will make progress because I've learned that what you tolerate, you eventually accept.

22

The difference between a lion and gazelle is that the lion is running toward something and the gazelle is running from something.

—Eric Thomas,
motivational speaker

I really enjoy contemplating the difference between these two animals, both running to survive, one to eat and one to be not eaten.

There's something appealing about this idea: working as hard as you can every day while always keeping in mind why you are traveling the path you've chosen. In the case of the two animals, both are working hard, but when the gazelle is no longer being chased, it stops running. Many times I've stopped running, because I've accomplished a goal. Or maybe I stopped doing my best, because I no longer had an audience. Yet experience has taught me I must always put in my best effort, even when no one is watching.

Maintaining one's work ethic requires honor and integrity. Working hard is often made easier when we know someone is watching us. Do you work hard and do the same level of detail-oriented work when you're alone as when you're observed?

I spent a lot of my life performing, so I knew when to switch it on and when to rest. There's a problem with that: my best self only emerged intermittently. Inconsistency breeds behaviors that marginally only improve your life. Run toward your goals daily, link your true purpose to something larger than yourself. This is crucial to staying on top of things.

The people who rely on me to be my best are a motivator I often consider, as, I think, most people do. Taking it a step further, however, helped me make motivation a constant in my life. So long as my mind and body are willing and able, I should know only hard work. Does anyone really wish to attain the highest version of themselves only when it is convenient or practical? I believe we have a social responsibility to wake up every day and be our best selves. People are counting on us, but a greater good comes from being able to live up to our own highest potential.

In a world in which people are always putting their best selves forward we all benefit. We cannot necessarily create a perfect society, but we can increase our chance to make good things happen. At times, the daily task of waking up to pursue what keeps us alive may seem a challenging task, but I'm confident it must carry a reward —lions are at the top of the food chain, after all.

23

It's okay to aim high and miss, but I'll have a real problem if you aim low and hit.

—Rick Rigsby,
journalist

In an amazing speech I heard, Rick Rigsby talked about his father. He said his father was the wisest man he had ever known. Although he had no formal education, he had learned many valuable lessons outside of the classroom.

For me, having high expectations was a terrible way to live my life. Until I was in my thirties I did the bare minimum needed to get by. I never thought it wrong to do things the easy way. I was working smarter, not harder. I also didn't see a lot of other people around me doing that. One of my friends went back to college, while a first-time mother I knew graduated with a bachelor's degree without telling anybody. I thought this was inspiring. The idea of working so hard and accomplishing something without making a huge deal about it seemed like something I could achieve.

I used to believe that if you want to achieve anything worthwhile in life, you had to tell everyone about it. That was my problem. I looked at achieving goals through the lens of the world's perceptions of my accomplishments. If I succeeded, it would reinforce my abilities, but it also meant I should do more. Remember, I thought I was

45

inherently lazy. More importantly, if I failed I would be able to tell myself, "stay in your lane" or "I told you so."

Fear of criticism held me back for many years. Even though I was achieving all the right things at an early age, I still believed my personal goals were far out of reach. When I managed to aim low and hit, I was disappointed but, unfortunately, accepted as normal. I always felt a lack of fulfillment.

I succeeded in aiming high—within the parameters of what I assumed other people expected of me, but I was afraid of aiming higher. One day, inspired by my friend who'd gone back to college, I decided to do the same.

When I changed my career path, I didn't announce it to the world. I just did it. I wanted to earn both a bachelor's and a master's degree. Strangely, I kept thinking I'd be ridiculed for these achievements. Instead I was congratulated and supported by those whose support was the most essential to me.

You can have a successful life even when you aim low and hit. But you won't be living the life of your dreams. Setting your sights high can be scary, but don't set yourself up for failure triggers. When your dreams are at stake, a mystical energy can emerge to trample simple motivation. Ignore the naysayers, especially if you yourself are among them.

24

*When you want something, all the universe
conspires in helping you achieve it.*

—Paulo Coelho,
The Alchemist

The journey of the main character in *The Alchemist*
revolves around a quest to find buried treasure.
Along the way, he meets many people who offer
him lessons, and he doesn't always know why he is
experiencing them. Ultimately, these lessons and the
stages of his journey become the path he must follow to
find the treasure.

A consistent theme of *The Alchemist* is following
one's dreams and remaining steadfast even when times
are tough and confusing. My own life is an example of
this. I've often been so focused on some final outcome
that I lose sight of what it means to get there.

Life rarely gives us a straight path to our goals. It's
easy to see everything that happens along the way as a
hindrance. I told myself that if my journey to a goal is not
a straight line, then clearly the world is telling me the path
is not for me. I should just quit.

How many times, when you've actually achieved
something, or learned a valuable life lesson, did you look
back along the path you took to get there and find it had
been straight and narrow? It seems to me now that the
more twists and turns I encounter on a journey, the richer
will be the final result.

Progress is most rewarding when you muster the energy to push forward despite difficulties. It's also a sweet feeling when you discover a strength and perseverance you didn't know you had; when every challenge holds the promise that you'll be able to overcome it.

If you're like me, you become angry and annoyed when many things get in your way. Maybe you curse yourself for going down a dumb path. However, regarding difficulties as "the universe attempting to prevent me from getting what I want" leads only to failure. Consider obstacles instead to be a necessary part of the singular pursuit of your dreams. You'll find it easier to accept them as temporary pains versus permanent troubles.

A new journey is often started with a goal in mind, but when the mini-victories and difficulties along the way are added in, there's a satisfying sense of achievement and self-growth in overcoming each challenge. Embrace the present instead of running from it. This allows you to embrace your setbacks. As Christian minister T. D. Jakes says, "before every blessing comes a lesson."

25

Start by cleaning your room.

—Jordan Peterson,
psychologist

Psychologist Jordan Peterson's point of view has been an invaluable influence on how I approach the world. He writes that people can do a tremendous amount of good for themselves and others around them by first addressing their own shortcomings and inadequacies.

Developing myself into a valuable person has indeed made me more useful to those around me, and may be the source of my positive influence on others. It's interesting how a simple act, such as cleaning your room or even just making the bed, can spark a larger chain of events to create positive change.

Like me, you might feel intimidated by taking on major tasks or challenges. In the past, I would avoid even starting. I would talk to others to reinforce my idea that not even trying is better. Some challenges can be daunting to tackle. Where does one even begin?

But daily discipline in making those decisions that actually help you get your life in order leads to growth. You become a better person, for you, your family, and your community. The rewards may even stretch beyond a local level.

After adopting this philosophy, I started noticing the people who don't have their own houses in order. It was not a judgment, but rather the simple observation that these people seem to believe themselves to be incapable of effecting meaningful change in their lives.

This philosophy has also made me wary of taking advice on how to live my life from others. Throughout our lives, bad things will happen. We always face challenges, but amid them, the one constant is our own self. It follows that our perception of the world, and our ability to effect change in it, are largely determined by being our own champions. When we hold ourselves accountable, when we start by getting the small things in our life in order, it creates a positive snowball effect, building and gaining momentum. We can aim every action toward a better future for ourselves and the people around us.

26

*The people that we let surround us either help us
to become the best version of ourselves
or encourage us to become
lesser versions of ourselves.*

—Robert Greene,
Mastery

Growing up in a large family and community,
I couldn't imagine not being surrounded by
dozens—maybe even hundreds—of friends and family
members, all of whom I would consider close. Throughout
my childhood, I viewed those around me as being close
to me regardless of my feelings for them; their mere
proximity was enough for me to consider them friends
or family.

This quote from *Mastery* challenged my view of
closeness, particularly of friendships. Is it possible that
only certain people have my best interests in mind?
Conversely, could it be that for some others, I was not
good for them? As time passed, it become apparent that
some people only wanted things from me, or worse,
wanted me to act in a particular way for their benefit.

Growing up as the funny kid, making people laugh
seemed to be what most people wanted. When I wasn't
funny, I was concerned my remarks might rub someone
the wrong way, even upset them. When I started to actively
put more energy into people who were committed to my
growth, I started to come more alive, like awakening from
a dream. The change was never about cutting people out
of my life. Rather, it's about focusing on people who are

51

open to the changes I seek in my life. Those who don't want me to change don't deserve my blame. I'm grateful for the opportunity to be of value to them in their lives, but in the long run, I can't offer them the same value.

I realize I may not have always reciprocated the encouragement I receive from others. This prompted me as an adult to approach friendship as a social contract, a contract to give as much of myself as I could to my close friends, because their support and encouragement are precious. It has become a daily mindfulness practice for me to ask myself if I've supported my friends as best I could. Or have I interacted superficially, with only the bare minimum of involvement? What was my contribution to bettering their lives? Engaging in the lives of those closest to you, supporting their growth and development, will inadvertently set the stage for your own growth and higher standards.

27

Your new life will cost you your old one.

—Jay Shetty,
British writer, life coach

Changing one's patterns of behavior is a bit scary at first. In order to receive something new, you first need to give something up. Jordan Peterson describes a similar concept using the analogy of burning off dead wood. Removing the parts of yourself that don't any longer serve—in your environment, relationships to people and things, and in your behavior—is necessary.

It's easy to argue whether this is a positive or negative sentiment. But your position in your own world is a telling indication. I had a lot of dead wood. In order to get to a better place in life, I have to endure moments that are not fun. I need to be honest with myself. I need to assess how much I don't like myself. Every action I take, every behavior I exhibit, contributes to a life I am not happy with. No matter how good the payoff is, part of me is afraid despite the ultimate payoff.

The experience of dealing with a life I didn't like gave me a sense of comfort, knowing I was well prepared to handle my own struggles. At a certain point, however, this pattern broke down. I realized that I wanted to change. This was an important stage. It marked the end of my old life.

To create a spark that pulls you toward something better, let go of old behaviors. I was good at marginalizing the gain of something new, because I had never actually had it before. But losing something, even if it was ultimately for the best, caused me fear and sadness.

In my life, I've often mistaken familiarity for value. In reality, I was suffering from a negativity bias. I focused more on potential negative outcomes than on positive ones. As the saying goes, life can be understood only by looking backward, but it must be lived by looking forward. There is no point in romanticizing the past. It must be taken with you. Gratitude acknowledges the circumstances and experiences that lead you to where you are in life. To overcome the fear of change, be grateful for the experiences you've had. Realize that you carry the best elements of your life into the next. It's an important—but beautiful—part of the journey.

28

People get upset not because of the adversity they face, but because their adversity reveals who they really are.

—Inky Johnson,
football player, motivational speaker

Hearing this for the first time can be kind of difficult, mainly because the words could not be more true for me. There is something about seeing a weak side of yourself that I absolutely hate. Let alone letting others see it, so I prefer to hide it or at least make it less conspicuous. In the face of your own insecurities, inadequacies, and negative self-talk, it's a difficult truth to face. There seems to be a generally defeatist attitude setting in, and all your hard work now seems to have brought you back down to a state of childlike inadequacy. But like a destructive tsunami passing through a coastal city, facing adversity can wash away everything not fastened down, leaving only a few standing structures.

You may consider yourself weak and useless at this moment, but those few structures that remain are elements that make you the strongest. I consider it to be a quote that reveals your true character, which for me wasn't one I was proud of; however, it can also help you recognize your inherent strengths. What remains when you're up against it reminds us that even though it's small, there is a part of you that shines resiliency and is worth restoring.

When you realize just how much work there is to be done to prepare for future storms, it can be a bit overwhelming, but it is an essential part of your self-development process. It doesn't matter if we are aware of it or not; you've been doing this for years, and each time you've weathered a storm, you've developed the ability to deal with future challenges. A stoic practice known as *negative visualization* is a valuable tool for keeping you focused on building up that area of yourself by reminding yourself of just how awful that moment of realization was and how you would never like to experience it again.

It's a revealing process, akin to the sculptor who chips away at marble to reveal the statue within. The imperfections and fractures in the stone are as integral to the final piece as its most exquisite features. Likewise, our flaws and failings, once acknowledged, do not define us; rather they offer us the truest sense of direction toward growth.

It's not about mourning the lost fragments or yearning for a past self that seemed invulnerable. The real strength lies in the steadfast structures that adversity couldn't topple. Do not spend too much time regretting who you thought you would be in that difficult moment and instead, choose to build upon your inherent capabilities so that the next time adversity knocks, you will answer confidently due to your strengthened abilities rather than shortcomings.

29

Our attitude towards others determines their attitude towards us.

—Earl Nightingale,
writer, radio personality

The golden rule encourages us to treat others as we want to be treated. The platinum rule tells us to treat others as they want to be treated. For the past fifteen years, I've had the opportunity to work with Fortune 500 companies. My experience tells me those in the business world prefer to be treated the way they want. When you treat others as they would like to be treated, you might think they'd reciprocate. Unfortunately, it's unlikely to happen. It's difficult, particularly in business, to deal with people who are cruel in pursuit of their own selfish ends.

I've encountered such behavior numerous times. It feels like people are taking and taking, until I am completely defeated and resentful. I couldn't help but think, what is the point of treating people well if they don't treat me well?

If you play the if-they-do-this-then-I'll-do-that game, you'll certainly fail. Trust me, I have tried everything. It's impossible to control the actions of another. Don't interact with people in a way that leaves you dependent on the actions of others to be happy. Find a way to be good to others without expecting anything in return. Find fulfillment in treating others how they want to be treated, because there's honor in living your life as the noblest version of yourself.

When I was part of these Fortune 500 companies, I witnessed people in positions of authority being completely awful to others. When others reciprocated in kind, it became an endless, negative cycle. What we can count on, however, is that if we are cruel to the world in the way we treat it, the world will almost always return the favor. This is the only certainty in the way we treat others.

30

*If you succeed at loving imperfect people,
then it becomes plausible that somebody
could love imperfect you.*

—T. D. Jakes,
non-denominational Christian preacher

It has been my own failing to build up resentment and use passive aggression toward people who bother me. My attitude arose from my own ego. I believed I was never to blame; it was always others who caused the problem. This cancerous trait destroyed many friendships, damaged family relationships, and nearly cost me my marriage. It's been said that the more time you spend with someone, the easier it is to notice their flaws over their good qualities.

In the same way, it's easier to notice the positive characteristics of someone when you first meet them. At some point I realized that neither view was accurate. Both situations require active concentration. When I enter into a new relationship, I tend to think it's somehow better than anything I've previously experienced. That may in fact be so, but it may also be that I am actively choosing to see the best in another. In a new relationship, it may seem that you're happier or bubblier than usual, but really, that has always been your natural state. A new relationship may simply be the catalyst that brings it out.

When you present your best self and search for the positive aspects of others, your entire outlook on life changes. It can seem as if everything just clicks into place.

Suddenly, the world is full of possibilities. As with any relationship, once the honeymoon phase has passed, it's easy to sense a lull. My marriage once showed traits I hadn't noticed before, and I wondered, were they always present? Was I blinded by the honeymoon phase? Did I really know this person? Ultimately, these are self-centered, narcissistic attitudes that lead to resentment. As with the good things that come in the beginnings of relationships, so also do bad things appear when you actively notice them.

At the time, I created my own narrative, in which my wife was responsible for all of my shortcomings. When I was unhappy, it was because of the way she was acting. When I wasn't growing in my career, it was because the very-motivated and hardworking me was defeated by this relationship.

It's possible to live in a world so upside down that those you love become the sole object of your resentment. Love, actually, is a choice. The honeymoon phase shows you a relationship's potential. As early attraction fades, it's up to you to be proactive. Work every day to keep your dream alive. It helps you see the best in another person if you practice mindfulness every day.

It's not easy to admit we're flawed. It's not just romantic to believe hard work keeps a relationship intact. It's dangerous to assume that by passively allowing things to run their course you will actually get the result you want. I know now that what I bring to a relationship has an immediate impact on our life together. Every day, I need to bring my best self to those I love. Only then can I count on reciprocity.

On waking up now, I practice actively recognizing my own shortcomings and making the choice to focus my energy on improving them. Regularly focusing on the positive aspects of the other person is crucial to nurturing the relationship. The honeymoon phase is, indeed, temporary, and that's a good thing, for what lies beyond it is far more valuable.

31

*There is no passion to be found playing small—
in settling for a life that is less than the one you
are capable of living.*

—Nelson Mandela,
South African anti-apartheid activist,
politician

Have you ever watched someone do something amazing and thought to yourself, that kind of thing is meant only for them or that certain accomplishments are reserved for an elite few? I have. Many times, I've watched others do great things but wrote them off for myself. To lead a comfortable life, it seemed a good idea to go for what I knew I could achieve. Neither playing big nor learning from failure were ingrained in me when I was a kid.

You can get to the island of safety with slow and steady diligence. There's nothing wrong with that. Despite minimal effort and minimal risk, I was able to showcase my own success in many ways, and it was often applauded by family and friends. Years passed before I understood that the applause created a limitation for me, reinforcing a lifestyle and behavior that did not produce fulfillment.

One day I heard that someone I'd grown up with had become an executive. It turned things around for me to hear this. I was not jealous, but seeing someone I'd grown up with achieve that kind of success changed my perspective on possibility.

Nobody in my world was expected to be able to achieve a success like that. We were expected to work steadily in mid-management jobs until retirement at the age of sixty-five.

I looked within my own ethnic group. How many Filipinos are in the top echelon of California's business community? I found it to be fewer than 0.2 percent. After seeing someone I knew succeed, I had to ask myself what I'm truly capable of.

Since then, I embarked on a journey to achieve the highest rank within my industry. I experienced the most significant achievements in my career during this time and expanded my professional network far beyond what I previously thought to be possible. In the five years since hearing about someone else's success, I've become an executive myself. Still, I've faced more failures than I can count. The personal growth I experienced and the bumps and bruises I acquired along the way have made each of these failures more fulfilling. I knew I was pursuing a life in line with my highest potential.

Aiming small and hitting can seem like a slow death. Knowing exactly what is around the corner all the time leaves little chance for excitement. To create the life you've always dreamed of, exchange the consistent success of playing small for the inconsistent failures that may actually lead you there.

32

As much as talent counts, effort counts twice.

—Angela Duckworth,
Grit

Growing up, I was surrounded by many talented people, but never thought I was particularly gifted at anything. Others excelled in sports, the arts, and academics, while I took an observer's role. Although I didn't see myself as talented in any one thing, I was known for my humor, so I considered that my gift. But I would never tell anyone just how much I worked at being funny. I studied others' behaviors when they said or did something funny. When I analyzed that person, I paid close attention to their tone of voice, body language, and even their timing. I developed my talent with years of practicing; I became known for my humor. But it wasn't until I read Duckworth's book that I realized a fundamental truth about talent and effort.

Although I didn't realize it at the time, my desire to create my own talent helped me develop a lifelong skill. Angela Duckworth talks about how effort and talent are not the same and that those who are inherently talented, but half as hardworking, will produce dramatically less over time. I used to think that only people with talents were blessed on this earth with certain opportunities in life and that since I didn't possess a talent, my life would be mediocre. My experience had been that those who showed great talent in childhood generally had the same outcomes as I did as a young adult, so inherent talent wasn't a predictor of their success.

Without hard work and consistent development over time, one's talent plateaus. In my case, my talent —humor—could take me only so far. Maintaining grit and consistency of effort over the long term is what makes all the difference. I believe anything you put your mind to can be reached at the same level as someone exceptionally talented in that field. There's more to it than the old adage, that you will become an expert in anything by simply logging 10,000 hours spent doing that thing, would suggest. It's not so much about how many hours you spend as it is the quality of those hours. It's developing the grit and perseverance to achieve a skill at the level that leads to success. Knowing your effort plays a major role in your growth and development is extremely liberating and opens a world of possibility.

33

The present is always changing the past.

—Alan Watts,
British writer, speaker

A lan Watts provides insight into how the past always flows back from the present. By analogy, he explains that you can only fully comprehend what is written once the sentence is completed. He goes on to say that you cannot change the past, but your perspective on it allows you to interact with your past in a more productive way.

Forgiving someone today for a past transgression won't change the past, but it will change the meaning you give to it. I have always held a great deal of resentment and anger for things that others have done to me in the past: I've also regretted the way in which I have treated others in my past. After discovering there is always a present that changes the past, I began to experience much-needed healing that I did not realize I needed. It can make you revisit old hurts, as well as the ways in which you might have hurt others.

Note that assigning new meanings to the past can be powerful. If you're like me, you've become adept at burying past experiences, never revisiting those memories. I thought just because I hadn't thought about an incident in a long time, it meant I was completely over it. I didn't realize just how exhausted I was making myself by pushing back unpleasant memories.

My aim today is always to make new chapters in my life. I give meaning to my past by living a life that makes use of all those experiences, leveraging them for a brighter future. I want to live a story of triumph in the now and use the past as fuel to make today's choices mindfully. Consequently, I can fully embrace what was in my past. In the process of "rewriting" the past, I am guiding my behavior today in order to adopt the behaviors I wish to see in myself.

Never underestimate the value of also incorporating the lessons you've learned as a gift back to the world. By doing so, you are able to assign meaning to every new experience in your life and bring it full circle.

34

Haters are a good problem to have. Nobody hates the good ones. They hate the great ones.

—Kobe Bryant,
pro-basketball player

Growing up as a fairly popular kid, I believed that if people hated you, it meant that you were "less than." As long as you were the same as everyone else, you were doing the right thing. It was a cool-kids'-club mentality, but sadly, a debilitating mindset that perpetuates a culture of uniformity. You don't dare shake up things, because that means you're ousted from your "tribe."

This is what my life was like as I headed toward college. It wasn't until I veered off the beaten path that I realized I could explore things that I really wanted to learn about. Unfortunately, not doing what was expected of me was causing tension in my family and friendships.

I think it's human nature to question why something is changing or to notice when something is out of the ordinary. The sad thing is that your friends and family will likely be the first to doubt your upcoming endeavors. When pursuing culinary school, for example, an endeavor not common in my family or group of friends, I perceived their reaction to be, "who are you to do this?"

Living your life solely to maintain the acceptance of those around you will make you invisible. It was Robert Greene, author of *Mastery,* who said "our desire for certainty is the greatest disease the mind can suffer."

There is a tendency to do things that are considered acceptable by others. When you pursue something you find meaningful in life, you must embrace everything that comes with it.

Generally, I tend to want the juice without the squeeze, but life doesn't always work that way. So, to Kobe's point, the great ones often get the most attention. Remember, as you become more visible in a crowd, it inevitably disrupts the people around you. That is okay. You must be able to go after what you want in life, even if those closest to you don't validate your dream.

When I started to operate from this mindset, everything changed. The ability to free myself from what others thought about me became my greatest asset. It is not necessary for others to believe in you or your dream. It's your own belief in your future that is crucial. When you no longer require validation or support from others, you'll be okay with the haters, because it's a signal that you're headed in the right direction.

35

The worst crime in the world is indecision.

—Sadhguru,
spiritual leader

I've always been one to put things off until later. Procrastination was a way of being. I thought there was a magical force inside me that would take over when I actually needed to make a decision.

But deciding not to decide is also a decision; I just didn't know it at the time. Indecision handcuffs your future by eliminating your power of choice. Making the decision to do something is scary for me. It is setting myself up for failure, I used to believe. I would say, "why even bother making a decision? If I don't achieve this, I will fail. Why put that type of pressure on myself today? Maybe tomorrow."

This was basically my philosophy of life, until I reached college. When all my friends had been accepted to state or university schools, and I found myself attending community college, my life philosophy came crashing down.

Although, there's nothing wrong with community college. I didn't even have a plan for that. When September rolled around, I needed something to do. I had made no plans.

Delaying a decision not only prevents you from progressing in life, it leads to things such as depression and feelings of inferiority. I came to realize the act of making a decision actually made me immensely happier. I learned that one decision leads to another. If you want to break out of a rut, you likely need to make some decisions. Then, take action. Do it, even if it does not seem like there is full clarity.

When my friends all went to college, I thought they had made their decisions right in the moment, in September. Turns out, it was years of making decisions that led them there. Each decision led to another, ultimately guiding them to choose a college. They decided not to play around in class (as I did). They made decisions: to do their homework, to research degrees, to explore universities. It's the process of decision-making that defines the path you'll ultimately walk.

Start by making a first decision. Then you'll make subsequent decisions. Each choice has a bit of wonder and mysticism to it. The beauty of this is, if you don't like the outcome, you can make another choice the next time.

When you eliminate indecision, momentum builds. I love this quote from poet John Keats: "Negative capability means we can pursue a vision even when it results in confusion and unpredictability rather than certainty." When you're open to possibilities, you suspend judgment and entertain all outcomes. This approach inspires you to embrace the unknown and the unfamiliar. For me, not knowing what a particular decision may lead to serves as a constant reminder that my often blurry future is worth pursuing verses living the very clear picture of the now.

36

I'm not Mother Teresa,
but I'm not Charles Manson, either.

—Mike Tyson,
professional boxer

I grew up in a middle-class family in a suburb, where I was certainly raised to be a kind person. As a child, I was generally friendly to others, even when I was bullied. I was basically a happy kid.

But after years of being kind to others seemingly without dependable reciprocation, anger, and resentment started taking a toll. In adulthood, I needed to relearn social norms. This time, I thought I needed to do what I had seen many others doing. People who were arrogant, selfish, and demeaning to others seemed to benefit, in both social and corporate settings. When I started expressing bad behavior, however, it was catastrophic. I felt good about being bad, and I felt a greater sense of satisfaction than I had ever experienced from being good. Bad behavior sparked more bad behavior, such as lying and stealing.

Keep in mind, I was a full-blown adult at this time, not a child. As a child, you're allowed to make mistakes. Your elders perhaps think that when you're older, you'll make better decisions. Embracing bad behavior is addictive. It is a gateway drug into increasingly bad habits. Subsequently, it changes neural pathways in the brain, increasing the probability you'll continue these behaviors.

My self-centered, narcissistic behavior not only made me depressed, it started to negatively affect my friends and family. But strangely, I became successful at work. Aggressive tendencies and manipulative behavior work wonders for climbing the corporate ladder. Success at work, however, was overshadowed by feelings of depression, loneliness, and—surprisingly—embarrassment for having achieved success. No amount of money or career accolades compensates for being unable to look yourself in the mirror. Neither being completely wholesome nor being abusive work well in life. It's useful to be able to bite back a little, just as it's useful to be nurturing. Yin and yang complement each other. Acknowledging that both exist within you is a form of self-acceptance.

Through this constant duality of good and bad, I've learned each day is a beautiful struggle. We're all just one decision away from adding more good or bad to the world. Choose wisely.

37

Do what makes you come alive.

—Howard Thurman,
theologian

Growing up, I had no idea what kind of career I wanted. I looked to my peers for inspiration. The only problem was, I wasn't actually looking for inspiration. I was simply looking for easy solutions. So I used other people's ideas. When college time came around, I used the dreams of others as inspiration to do the same, telling myself that if they would choose to do something, believing it would make them happy, then why not me?

I chose a career in culinary arts. On paper, it looked amazing. My grades were excellent. I had cooked in some of the best restaurants in the area. By most measures, I was successful in the kitchen. However, when it came to the most creative part of the cooking process—the plating—I failed. I could find no passion in this process. I was simply tossing food on a plate. I was almost upset that the cooking process was over. My peers, however, seemed to find joy in the plating. I wondered why I wasn't enjoying it.

This is when I started to see the impact of doing something for the wrong reasons. Even if it brings you success, the moment all the glamour fades, you're left with what's in front of you. If it's not something you want to do on even your worst days, it can be an empty moment, full of regret.

Having spent years in culinary arts, I was surprised when I was called into a meeting with management one day. They seemed to think I had developed great relationships with everyone in the kitchen, but I was not a great cook. They saw me as a natural leader and communicator. They wanted to put me into a role better suited for my talents—kitchen management. I had little passion for restaurants, but I discovered I did have a talent for problem solving. In management, everything is about solving problems. In retrospect, I didn't love the life of a chef. I didn't even enjoy going to fancy restaurants. I did love cooking itself. I liked turning raw ingredients into a beautiful dish.

To this day, I am driven by problem solving. I have since searched for career opportunities that involve solving problems. Cooking meant taking raw ingredients and transforming them into something special. It was, in fact, my analogy for problem solving. I saw concept of cooking and management through the lens of my core passion: the drive to create.

I also had a passion for marketing. Take, for example, an account that is losing money. I like to turn such an account into a cash cow through marketing. What's important is the connection between the product and customer. My marketing job gives me the opportunity to wake up each day and find solutions to problems. This is not necessarily a romantic notion, and many would argue it is too much work. Why work so hard?

My passion for solving problems is a highly valuable skill in corporate America. I increased my market value almost four-fold when I honed my skills as a problem solver.

The pursuit of problem solving is something I hope to do until the day I die, not for the sake of financial gain, but because it offers fulfillment that money cannot provide.

38

I'm not afraid to look like an idiot.

—Anthony Bourdain,
chef, restauranteur

Have you ever seen someone do something completely out of the ordinary? You were sure it would end in disaster, but in the end, it worked out. And the crowd (if there is one) erupts in applause and cheers. This has happened to me a few times. Growing up as a class clown and voted "the most talkative," I felt I had to continually one-up my last feat in order to continue holding status and acceptance. I had to come up with outrageous, innovative ways to make people laugh again and again. It had to be something people would talk about.

I didn't do these things for a great reason, but they did teach me a valuable lesson that continues to be relevant in my life. As soon as I was ready to do something really important to me, I felt like I was standing on a cliff, waiting to dive into the deepest water. As soon as the moment presented itself, and I jumped, I was in a state of bliss. Taking chances that others wouldn't take gives me a sense of freedom. Knowing that you're heading into the unknown creates a euphoric rush of adrenaline.

People didn't really seem to care if I succeeded or failed. The mere fact that I attempted something was enough. The acceptance of my peers followed, but the real treasure was the boost of confidence that came with doing something that scared the living crap out of me.

People still reminisce about things that happened when I was a ten-year-old. The more you let go of whatever you're afraid of, the better the chance you'll live an extraordinary life.

Dealing with life's challenges offers a friendly reminder that no matter the outcome, simply taking action is enough. You may eventually get what you want—praise, promotions, riches—but those things are fleeting. Their lasting effects depend on what really matters to you. In the process, momentum builds to where you no longer hesitate, but act immediately. The real treasure is what jumping makes of you. If you think about people who have succeeded in life, you notice they all punted the system. As entrepreneur Gary Vee says, the risk is worth it.

39

Don't wish for fewer challenges,
wish for more wisdom.

—Earl Schoaff,
entrepreneur, motivational speaker

The late Jim Rohn was a student of Earl Schoaff, who reminds us that seasonal change is inevitable. Winter will always come, but don't wish it was summer. We have to suffer through the cold to get to the sunny days that follow. This is a great metaphor for highlighting an obvious principle: life's struggles are seasonal.

The issue this quote identified for me was my laziness. The weather is easy to blame in a case where things just aren't working out. You have the most reasonable excuse, because in one sense you are not wrong about it. There truly are challenges that present themselves. They come and go continuously.

Often when I'd reminisce about the past, I could recall only a few months of easy times—the summers as it were —where everything went my way. Hard times are more difficult for me to remember without active concentration. For me, life would stop when I faced struggles. Rather than fight back, I wallowed in self-pity until the sunny days returned. I was lazy. When things got tough, I'd curse my fate for being stuck with it.

This is a poor man's way of living and looking back. I used to live life a few months at a time. Worse, those around me reinforced my circumstances. Don't get me wrong: there are times in life when it is helpful to be surrounded by those who empathize with your struggles, especially when you are facing death and illness.

Figuring out what I can do to prepare myself for challenges is a daunting task. Who really wants to spend so much time forecasting their future, and putting in the grueling work to prepare for it? It's the reason why fewer than 60 percent of Americans are prepared for retirement. Even though we know the hard times are coming, we just turn a blind eye and hope for the best. You can clearly see the coming winter and yet you do nothing about it. This approach to life will hit you twice.

At first, you'll be upset that you're faced with another challenge. Your frustration is then compounded by the realization that you could have done something when it was clearly coming your way. We're responsible for many of life's challenges; our own behaviors contribute to accelerating the approaching winter. By identifying negative tendencies and behaviors in advance, you prepare yourself and stand a better chance of overcoming life's constant challenges.

40

See the bagel.

—Simon Sinek,
writer, motivational speaker

Following a race, distance runner Simon Sinek and a friend get free bagels. But there's a long line of runners waiting to get their free post-race treat. After seeing the line, his friend says the wait is too long and doesn't wait. At that point, Sinek saw there were two ways to perceive the world. Sinek saw only the bagel, while his friend saw only the line. We can see the thing we want or we can see the thing that stands between us and what we want.

There have been a lot of times in my life when I didn't go for what I wanted, because I was focused on what was in the way. It's why I didn't try harder in school; it was simply too much work to get an "A." I didn't try harder in sports, because building my body's athleticism would just be too hard. Why start now, I asked myself.

I didn't decide to go to college for more than a decade after I graduated from high school. Although the path of least resistance is a practical way of getting through life, the sad truth is that most will do just that, get through life.

David Goggins, a former Navy SEAL, describes a process of "callousing" your mind. When you're overwhelmed by current challenges, it's easy to lose perspective on what you want. What's the point? Why put yourself through it? Is it worth the effort? In keeping your sights on what you want, you learn to accept and often look forward to the opportunities life presents along the way. In my thirties, I became aware I could do more. There is no doubt in my mind I have accomplished more in the last few years than I did in the preceding two decades. I finally started experiencing what life could be like if I really made an effort to pursue my deepest desires. It's not easy. You will get hurt, heartbroken, and experience failures, but ultimately you'll win. It may not look as you imagined, but the road less traveled offers undreamed of treasures. It's the unexpected gifts along the way that make the journey worthwhile.

I found the true gift is not what I've achieved but who I became. I value the deep bonds formed with those who supported me on my journey. In the long run, it is fantastic to attain what you desire. Developing the skill of confronting and overcoming adversity in the process is equally valuable.

41

Real integrity is doing the right thing, knowing that nobody's going to know whether you did it or not.

—Oprah Winfrey,
talk show host, producer

As a child, having a few quarters in my pocket made me feel rich. As we drove home from day care one day, I sat next to my sister and watched her count the money in her wallet. I was envious because she had, not quarters, but dollar bills. I asked her to offer me one of her many dollars, and she did so quickly, without hesitation.

I was completely shocked. If she had asked me for a dollar, I would not have given her one. Or if I had, I would've made sure the world saw my holy gesture. I might even have lied, saying, "sure, I'll give you a dollar when we get home," with no intention of actually doing it. My sister actually just offered me one of her dollars. It's a memory that will always be with me, of doing something you say you will do for someone else without expecting praise or admiration in return. My sister taught me three lessons that day. She taught me to be genuinely kind to other people. She taught me to do good things without expecting something in return. And she taught me to be true to my word.

Still, it took almost a decade to realize I needed to incorporate such traits into myself. I spent years honing those of my skills that got me what I wanted, without a shred of regret. If the essence of integrity is doing what is right whether or not anyone knows about, then the contrary is also true. Accepting unearned praise leaves you feeling hollow inside.

When I was living with little integrity, I didn't care if I won by cheating or lying. Living this way breeds the worst in people, and I was no exception. I became sick of myself by the time I was in my twenties. I was convinced that this was just who I was. Seeing people with integrity around me made me wonder if they were born with something I wasn't.

Everything changed when I met my wife. She was a woman with character and solid values that she lived by. She's the type of person who saves the last piece of pizza, wraps it up, and offers it someone who hasn't eaten. It was a quality that drew me to her. The quote about integrity from Oprah describes my wife. It's one of the biggest reasons I love her. I wanted a life filled with traces of such kind traits.

More than a decade later, I discovered that surrounding myself with those who carry themselves with integrity is the key to finding my own. Integrity is a gateway to our highest self. Not getting credit for something when you deserve it can be hurtful, but living with undeserved praise will break you. You must realize how little you embody a trait before you will ever want to cultivate it for yourself.

42

The chief cause of failure and unhappiness is trading what you want most for what you want right now.

—Zig Ziglar,
writer, motivational speaker

As an adult, I have come to appreciate the benefits of delaying gratification. As the youngest of three, I learned the lessons my older siblings had learned before me. I took full advantage of the "third child syndrome" —the time and energy my parents devoted to my older siblings was lost on me. I was free to do as I desired; my parents just didn't seem to focus much attention on me. On the other hand, my parents' praise and affection grew when I began to demonstrate some important behaviors.

As the saying goes, what comes quickly doesn't usually have value, and what has value usually doesn't come quickly. Some values I had had as a youth began to crumble when I reached adulthood. When I entered college, I realized I had never developed a strong work ethic. I carried a fundamental misunderstanding of how the world worked. Simply put, I had been spoiled. Now, it was time to pay the piper.

I spent years as an adult learning things other kids had learned as children. Particularly patience. My perception of what it really takes to earn something was skewed, because I seemed able to get what I wanted without any real difficulty.

At first, I thought my school schedule was extremely demanding or my work too hard. Not the case. I was just lazy. It's human nature to ask the universe for the things we want now, hoping that they will somehow bring us happiness and fulfillment. But living a life of unearned abundance ends up giving us the opposite of what we desire. Fulfillment comes from earning rewards.

In the classic tale of King Midas, when everything is gold, nothing is precious. The act of sacrificing today for tomorrow seems to be a test of patience. It's a boost of confidence when you realize you don't have to wish for what you want; you have only to work hard to get it. When you're grateful for what you have, it's empowering to be able to rely on yourself to achieve your future. It is more of an exception than a rule that you will receive all that you desire in life, at the exact moment you wish for it. Delayed gratification is the only guaranteed method of obtaining everything you desire.

43

*When you judge another, you do not define
them, you define yourself.*

—Wayne Dyer,
writer, motivational speaker

Growing up, I'd always judged others. In retrospect,
my judgments were often based on things they
could do that I couldn't. To temporarily alleviate my self-
deprecating feelings, I would actively seek out situations
where I could be the best at something. As I've mentioned
before, my way of overcoming my low self-esteem was
being the funniest person in the room. But as I've also
mentioned before, being funny was no longer useful
to me after a while as other things, such as my grades,
my work ethic, and my physical fitness, became more
important.

I was once pretty upset about how my sense of humor
—which I'd spent years cultivating—gradually came to
seem pointless. I was constantly comparing myself to
others who had inherent abilities and talents. It would be
easy, seeing the lives of others, to think they are simply
gifted. My beliefs were bred by envy and resentment. If I
was the funny guy who didn't get good grades and wasn't
athletic, then so be it. I would be begrudgingly as funny
as possible.

It took me years to realize I can do whatever I
choose to do. When I judged others, I was projecting my
own insecurities. The only person we should compare

ourselves to is ourselves, judging only where we are in comparison to where we were yesterday. My relationship with judgment has changed for the better. I remind myself today not to be resentful or envious, but to be inspired, because I was able to recognize in myself something I wished to achieve.

When you judge others, you amplify your own insecurities, and many people would agree that social media doesn't help when you have this type of behavior. The realization only came to me a few years ago that I could use social media as inspiration and not as a source of judgemental resentment. Over the years, I have often compared my point A with another's point B.

The relationship I have with judgment has changed for the better today, and I think of it as a reminder that whatever I'm judging others for, it's time to notice that something has awakened inside me.

Because judgment is addictive in many ways, and does offer some satisfaction, it will always be temporary and shallow. Whether it is changing an unhealthy behavior or starting a new adventure, this is a solemn reminder that you need to do some work on yourself. Continuing to do it the old way will eventually bring you to the edge of change over and over again, and there is nothing worse than seeing what might have been and doing nothing about it.

44

No longer chasing butterflies, Camila and I planted our garden so they could come to us.

—Matthew McConaughey,
actor

As someone who looks to the future, it's easy for me to be captivated by what lies ahead. Seeing today is just a steppingstone to tomorrow's successes. I once heard someone say, there is only the eternal present. This upset me for some reason. I never wanted to be in the present. For me, it was a begrudging task, living through today to get to tomorrow.

In my current life, I can get caught between procrastination and an attitude of victimization. I've often spent time chasing what isn't there, instead of believing I can actually create what I want.

The quote from Matthew McConaughey inspires me to stop chasing what's not here and, instead, build something amazing, right here and now. As an adult, I now understand why I didn't want to do that for so many years. It was because I was unhappy with myself for being lazy. I knew chasing butterflies was easier than growing a garden, but when I wanted to try something new or difficult, I was too lazy to do it. Why would I spend any time building a garden when I could be imagining the amazing garden and butterflies I would have one day.

Then I began to focus on my closest family and friends, and my life started to really blossom. I had often neglected this special group, not realizing they had always been the garden. They are the ones who stand by me through thick and thin. They have no expectations of who I need to be tomorrow.

There are treasures all around us if we just look closely enough. The grass is always greener when it's watered.

Because I have spent my entire life chasing butterflies, so to speak, it is not surprising that I have missed the garden in which I was already running around, admiring another's lush garden rather than maintaining my own.

Throughout my life, I dreamed of a world other than the one I live in now. That my future was a completely different place, a faraway land, where everything, including me, was different. If you can look around yourself, invest in what you can in what is in front of you, and the garden will grow, you don't necessarily need to stray off into a faraway land or hope that your fulfillment will come one day in the distant future.

Those butterflies you sought so earnestly will find their way to you. Even if you don't see butterflies right away, you will begin the process of attracting all the things that you desire in life, if you direct all of your energy toward simply attending to what's immediately front of you.

45

*If you met the person you were capable of being
on your deathbed, would it be like you're looking
in the mirror or a meeting a stranger?*

—Ed Mylett,
entrepreneur

Entrepreneur Ed Mylett calls the twenty-one-day work week a method to triple productivity. A day is twenty-four hours, but we generally refer to a normal workday of eight hours, which, if we're honest with ourselves, is only a few hours of actual productivity. To maximize productivity, Mylett suggests doing those productive actvities in a specific time frame. His approach is to divide a twenty-four-hour day into three mini-days. He schedules his first day between 6 A.M. and noon, his second day between noon and 6 P.M., and his third day between 6 P.M. and midnight.

Consider monitoring the progress of your day. Being hyper-focused, sticking only to what you set out to do, may seem exhausting. But being focused is likely to bring about positive change.

This is actually the opposite of being busy. It's somewhat calming to know that, for the next few hours, you'll do only one particular task, and nothing else. This allows you to concentrate on what's right in front of you. It's like an escape from everything else.

The first time I applied Ed Mylett's framework, my productivity skyrocketed. I saw solid results. But, when I don't remain focused, I end up getting stuck and not taking action. I had several goals. To be a better husband, get a promotion at work, get a degree, and to compete in something fitness-related. I had no idea how to actually accomplish all of this. After adopting Mylett's framework, my first day began with rising at 3:30 A.M. My goal for the first day was fitness. First, I turned my attention to getting the dishes done, cleaning up the house, and preparing lunches for the kids. These needed to be done by 4:30 A.M. so I could take advantage of a CrossFit or Olympic weightlifting session.

I would then be able to start my second day, which was devoted to my career, taking on new projects for my leadership. Finally, I spent my evenings, or third day, on family and personal growth, enjoying quality time with my wife and kids, and finished off with two hours of schoolwork. I would finally go to bed around 10 P.M., getting about six hours of sleep.

Despite what people might think, this was not a lifestyle full of chaotic deadlines and schedules; it was the exact opposite. Intentionality with time is one of the greatest gifts you can give to yourself. I treat each day as a twenty-four-hour mission.

My relationship with my wife and kids is now the best it has ever been. I've earned multiple degrees, participated in national weightlifting competitions, and doubled my income. The idea that anything you wish to achieve in life is possible becomes tangible as a result of this concept. Knowing that you're doing everything you can be doing empowers you. I had always looked to the future, never wanting to see what the actual road to get there looked like. My only hope was to pray for productive days. When that happened, it was sheer dumb luck.

You will waste your life away in the blink of an eye waiting for these moments to come. Also, it's not about what you accomplish. Your relationship with time also changes. Making time an ally will give you a tool to accomplish all you want in life.

46

Make it your daily obsession
to make the most of your potential.

—Tom Bilyeu,
co-founder of Quest Nutrition

As someone who has lived a life of just getting by, I learned that doing the bare minimum is an art. As strange as it may seem, doing the minimum involves more effort than you might think. You have to visualize the entire end-to-end process, then peel back each layer, and all those things make it challenging and hard. In order to find the right balance of bare minimum effort, you'll need to add a few things back in, to ensure it hits just the right level of achievement. The art lies in self-deception: that others will give you maximum praise for your minimal effort.

I would do the bare minimum out of fear that doing more would interfere with my busy schedule of doing nothing. I did this in all aspects of my life. It was fine for me to exercise just enough to not be overweight, to do just enough work to not be considered lazy, to attend friends' birthday parties but stay only for dinner, to prepare a big celebration for my wife's birthday but neglect the daily attention leading up to it. "We become what we repeatedly do, so excellence is not an act, it is a habit," as American historian and philosopher Will Durant once put it.

Though this quote was inspiring, it reminded me that you can live a selfish life, where things are easy and undeserved praise leaves you somewhat gray. By not fully investing yourself in anything, you never fully experience life.

My expectations of my lazy workouts came crashing down one year, when I received bloodwork that showed I had high cholesterol. My one-sided friendships failed to be long-lasting. Neglecting my marriage caused me to become distant from my wife. Putting forth minimal effort ensures you'll know exactly where you'll end up and what you will and won't accomplish. It leaves little room for what life can offer you if you put forth the effort.

A breakdown offers an opportunity for each of us to reach the next level of understanding. I used to believe that making a mark on the world required grand gestures. I've learned that making the most of my abilities is a sequence of small actions. Becoming a more attentive husband, writing down what I've eaten, or being the first to reach out to a friend; these may go unnoticed by others, but they are the bedrock on which I build lasting habits that benefit my life. Accepting the minimum is like making a rapid, easy descent; accomplishing the many small, daily tasks is like a slow, steady ascent.

Applying effort to all things in your life requires diligence and hard work. As the great philosopher Mahatma Gandhi said, "Every worthy act is difficult."

Today I take the time to be mindful of each thing I'm focused on and ask myself, could I be doing more? The answer is almost always yes. I then envision how my higher self would feel if I had done that one extra small thing, and it propels me into action knowing that I am capable of better. Take every moment seriously, throughout your life, while doing difficult things day in and day out. It undermines your lesser self and creates an avenue to realize your highest potential.

47

*The only time you should look back in life
is to see how far you have come.*

—Kevin Hart,
American comedian, author

In both of Kevin Hart's books, he describes how his parents influenced him and his brother in very different ways. Kevin's brother was raised in violence and crime, much like his father. But Kevin's mother tried her best to steer him away from these paths. This meant Hart was shadowed by his mom at every turn. Every minute of the day, he was busy, with school, swimming, walking, or taking public transportation all over town with his mother, who did not believe they should be a burden on anyone.

He didn't realize at the time that how his mother raised him developed in him a strong work ethic, patience, and humility. Those values laid the foundation for his famous work ethic and for his global fame. I enjoyed reading about his upbringing, because it reminded me of my own upbringing but also that of friends who were the youngest of their families. As children, we were all constantly swept up in family activities.

Growing up I wanted more control over my life. I was forced to attend sports practices and music practice. I begrudgingly did chores and yard work, without realizing the lasting values that my parents were instilling.

Today I appreciate the process of working hard. When the work is over, and you have the rewards of success, you look back on those moments and value them the most, Hart said. Before reading his books, I had no idea Hart performed stand-up comedy all over the East Coast for next to nothing or that he had so many failures in television and movies. I had no idea that he was still struggling. At that point, he didn't realize he was making it; all he was doing was repeating the daily grind that he had been living for the previous five years. That was the part of his story that I enjoyed the most, because it demonstrated how his upbringing gave him a foundation to succeed.

For me, working as hard as possible, day in and day out, is almost a noble endeavor with no clear finish line. When you're not concerned with the ultimate outcome or where you are in the process of achieving your dream, you almost feel nirvana. The most important thing is to keep working hard, because today's efforts build upon yesterday's efforts.

The expectation of immediate gratification has become so prevalent today. Being in the process is somehow a losing proposition. I believe being in the process is the highest form of self-achievement. Getting up every morning and working as hard as you can is the best way to ensure success in the long run.

According to popular talk show host Oprah Winfrey, "one must not judge a day by what one reaps, but by how many seeds one planted." Having this appreciation for the journey and its daily hard work requires a personal paradigm shift for many of us. Even though it is not glamorous, it is fundamentals such as character, values, and discipline that prove most valuable in the end. It is almost blissful to lose yourself in the grind. When the time finally comes that you've achieved your goal, you can look back and see where you have come from. Your progress will be more than adequate, arguably more fulfilling than the achievement itself.

48

Maturity is the ability to reject good alternatives in order to pursue even better ones.

—Ray Dalio,
American billionaire,
hedge fund manager

Frequently, the idea that life is painful is thrown around. In this philosophy, any relief we can obtain should obviously be taken as soon as possible. Many times that's exactly what each of us does. I have had my fair share of indulgent moments, the immediate gratification of which usually ended up being fleeting, forgotten just as quickly as they appeared.

Certainly, the idea of delayed gratification is not trendy these days. With the use of social networks, we're bombarded with so much information about what so many people are achieving, what so many others are accomplishing, or where so many have already arrived.

Ray Dalio is one of the most successful investors of all time. He reinforces the point that today, working hard is by far the best way to set up your future self for the self-fulfillment you desire in the present. In this case, the good alternatives would be the easy way out, but these will leave you with "empty calories" that do not give you the satisfaction you're seeking.

I have had situations in my past where I went for and gained exactly what I wanted right then and there, only to find it was a short-lived experience. Acting on impulse,

I achieved nothing and was now back at the beginning, wanting once more.

Every time you face something painful, you are at a potentially critical juncture in your life. You can choose between the healthy-yet-painful truth or the unhealthy-yet-comforting delusion. Delusion is the inability to accept the fact that achievement of any goal in life is always accompanied by difficulties and challenges. An unhealthy delusion is like a spell, cast by your lower self, pleading with you to end your suffering and trade what you most strongly desire right now. It is similar to building a muscle. You must be able to recognize that moment when you decide to deviate from your goal.

The reason people don't stick to their plans is because their motivation isn't compelling, or they have too little of it. The importance of Why should be so strong that it wakes you up in the morning and prevents you from sleeping in. It is the underlying reason you aspire, something beyond the reward, a mission, something that stirs you and will not detour you from your goal.

To avoid acting on impulse, inspirational speaker Tony Robbins recommends we use positive distractions such as healthy behaviors to keep us on task. The Whys that we've developed and the healthy behaviors we've adopted keep us focused and will enable you to live a life in which the only temporary thing will be the suffering you encounter on the way.

49

Guilt is a wasted emotion.

—Iyanla Vanzant,
American writer,
inspirational speaker

Guilt and shame, we are told, are cousins. In my experience, guilt is the gateway to shame, if I don't deal with it. As the youngest of three siblings, I knew a world where I often got my way. As I got older, I did things to ensure this state of affairs continued. I didn't see my actions as evil, merely as a means of getting my way.

When I was growing up, my moral compass was absent. The rules did not apply to me. Small lies were here and there, as were cheating on tests and stealing things of little value. I asked myself, what's the harm? I'm not hurting anyone; why is it so bad? After years of doing this even as an adult, I now recognize guilt is the gateway to shame. It's not so much that I would get caught doing something bad, but rather that the bad inside of me only grows. It's cancerous. Eventually, it gets so large that shame takes over and it becomes easier to continue living the lie than it is to admit it.

For years, I dealt with shame from things I did as a child, adolescent, and young adult. Those moments when I was completely consumed with myself, when I did things only to achieve my selfish ends. I recognize myself in the Johnny Cash song *Hurt,* where he talks about wearing a crown of thorns, sitting in his liar's chair, and wanting to give away his empire of dirt.

I remember vividly not liking who I was as a person. It was a humbling moment. I wanted nothing to do with these bad behaviors and traits. I felt disgust for who I was and how I got to be the man I was. I saw my own successes but questioned whether I'd have gotten there if I hadn't stepped on so many people, hadn't cheated the system. I doubted whether I'd have achieved the same results.

When you realize that your actions and words are not in alignment, that is the moment your life will begin to change. Doing away with your past self begins by telling yourself enough is enough. Guilt is a wasted emotion. You cannot change the past. But you can use the past as a compass to stop making the same mistakes over and over. You cannot change the things you regret but you can recognize they've happened. So what should you do next?

It's frightening to think about losing everything, even if it's to regain yourself. Obtaining what I wanted by the easiest means possible, however, was the slow death of my character that rendered all my accomplishments meaningless and unfulfilling.

The practice of recalling my past behavior helps me act mindfully today, so as not to repeat past mistakes. Releasing your past karmic ties by making amends for past mistakes requires a commitment to new behaviors. Maintaining a healthy relationship with your mistakes is the most valuable part of your experience, the exact playbook you must follow to avoid repeating them in the future.

50

*Say thank you in advance
for what's already yours.*

—Denzel Washington,
actor

Of all the gifts I've encountered that have helped me make my life better, gratitude has by far been the greatest. A practice of daily gratitude was often mentioned by those I was reading and listening to, starting in 2017. The idea of faking happiness, (because you can always imagine things being worse), never interested me much. I considered it an illusion. In my mind, what I was dealing with at that moment was still something I disliked, regardless of the possibility that things could be worse elsewhere. What was the point of being grateful for it?

I was absolutely wrong in my philosophy of life. I was always focusing on the problem at hand, not on what wasn't the problem. Simple as that. Because you can't control what happens in your life, it's easy to become hyper-focused on your immediate circumstances. By concentrating only on the negative, the problem becomes an outlet for expressing all your fears, anxieties, and anger.

An absence of gratitude distorts your life perspective and allows you constantly to find more reasons to be unhappy. Being ungrateful creates a snowball of negativity. On the other hand, practicing daily gratitude can have a magnifying effect. Find one thing you're thankful for each day, and you'll start to feel better about yourself.

Starting with something simple, such as a cup of coffee, I observed my gratitude and started to notice how my day was starting with a smile. I noticed the cup, the kitchen, the house, and most importantly, my beautiful wife and amazing children. It didn't take me long to remember that my parents were still around and that my best friends and siblings were only a phone call away.

Starting small allowed me to experience more positive emotions and appreciate past experiences. Ultimately, it created a sense of empowerment against the storms I was experiencing.

When I first heard Tony Robbins talking about gratitude as a solution to anger and fear, it was a foreign idea for me. Now I realize anger and fear can't flourish when I don't give them a platform. In no way does gratitude make life easier or make problems disappear. It simply changes how you perceive problems. That in turn facilitates a more positive and empowered approach to solving them.

Consider the ease of having a "woe is me" attitude around friends, family, or coworkers. There is little chance of chaos and cynicism disappearing, so writing down a daily gratitude is like fortifying yourself in the midst of a battle.

As you begin to build a daily gratitude practice, you realize there are many things you can draw from, an infinite well of positive perspectives applicable to all situations in life. For years, my arrogance and entitlement caused me to be resentful toward the challenges in my life. I felt grateful only when something of monumental proportion came my way. Even then, my gratitude was fleeting. If you can't find fulfillment or happiness in the now, you'll never find it, no matter what you achieve. Developing a habit of gratitude makes today even more precious and tomorrow even more promising, a constant reminder that you're fortunate to already be living yesterday's better tomorrow.

51

*Stop planning to get to 100 percent
and instead take the 2 percent action.*

—Evan Carmichael,
venture capitalist,
YouTube influencer

Whenever you consider making a major change in your life, it's easy to get stuck in analysis paralysis. At work, I'm rewarded for meticulously planning, analyzing, and forecasting my every move. So why shouldn't I do the same with my own life? The problem with planning is that it's never finished. Everything is subject to change. Things can always be improved. Practicing gratitude is always a work in progress. Don't let it become an excuse to never begin anything new.

Planning forever also allows you to avoid failure. You never try; therefore you never succeed. It is true that if you try, you increase your chances of failure, but if you don't try, you're guaranteed to achieve only a single certainty. You will not achieve what you desire.

Every worthwhile endeavor involves a healthy dose of fear. As trite as it sounds, though, failing fast and falling forward is the only way to see progress in your life. Evan Carmichael mentions a 2 percent action, which I have certainly dismissed as useless. Who wants to start with a baby step? I was unwilling to do so for fear of looking foolish, because the new things I wanted to try were simply not meant for me.

Starting with 2 percent may seem insignificant, but it represents a 100 percent shift in mindset that will accompany your new behavior. The empowerment you feel from taking a 2 percent action is a catalyst that enables you to keep moving toward your goal. Once you've started, you're less likely to give up, just by sheer inertia. According to experts, the vast majority of rocket fuel is used when the rocket is launched. It is a misconception that the amount of effort applied at the beginning of a journey must be applied throughout. It actually becomes easier the more effort you put forth.

I often say that starting small is the way forward, but the only word in that phrase that really counts is starting. I've discovered that even though there are risks of failure all along the way, casting your own dreams aside and choosing a path of fear disguised as practicality is the biggest failure. The decision to live for the sake of practicality is the handcuffs that shackle your dreams. There are times when your closest friends and family members will confirm the risks and the necessity of practicality, because they don't want you to be disappointed or hurt. There will be pain, either in the form of suffering en route to your goals or in dwelling upon the hurt and disappointment that you could have done more, but you deliberately chose not to.

52

Eventually you will see that the real cause of problems is not life itself. It's the commotion the mind makes about life that really causes problems.

—Michael A. Singer,
The Untethered Soul

My love of planning my day and checking off everything I accomplished had made control a way of life. Normally, I spent most of my days being upset that things weren't going according to plan.

Michael Singer teaches that much of life unfolds due to forces outside of our control. We simply experience it. Our consciousness determines our perceptions of it. I like the idea that I really don't have any reason to be upset about the way my life is going, but this was not an easy concept for my control-freak mind to accept. I thought it would be akin to giving up on life, to just passively let life take its course. In fact, it's the opposite. It helps reinforce the notion that what comes your way will come your way. How you perceive it is up to you.

We are influenced by our inner voices. If you're anything like me, your inner voice is something of an asshole. I often hear my subconscious telling me that I'm not good enough, I'm useless, I make irrational decisions. It taunts me—"I told you so"—at the worst possible times.

For many of us, inner voices get prime real estate in our heads. They are not held accountable for prompting bad decisions. We have no trouble listening to them again the next time around.

Staying in the present is a skill that must be developed daily. It allows you to distinguish between what is really happening around you and what you are just telling yourself about what's happening. Many people—myself included—spend their days trying to protect themselves and ensure that nothing goes wrong.

By expecting life to be a certain way, we place heavy expectations on the world that are unlikely to be met. Furthermore, painting in your mind an overly specific picture of what life should look like leaves no room for how life might evolve. It eliminates the beauty and surprises life offers.

I developed patterns of avoidance over the years, but all it did was increase my isolation from the world. I believed life was conspiring against me. It was a good day when I made it through with no injuries or disappointments and everything had gone as planned.

Going with the flow of events or emotions is not passive; it's empowering. I learned that allowing events or emotions to flow through me is a type of freedom. Being completely open to how life unfolds, then implementing this understanding of positive perception, I now realize life doesn't happen to me, it happens for me. Because we can choose our own way of experiencing life, upholding our consciousness offers us the freedom to do so.

53

Play hard, work harder.

—50 Cent,
American rapper, entrepreneur

Learning that 50 Cent packs his laptop first when going on vacation was something that resonated with me. I do the same thing. When I'm on vacation, I think about work. I've always enjoyed it especially when I'm on vacation, so when retirement discussions came around, I didn't want anyone to know I didn't feel the same way they did. The aim of my life was always to make money, so I could retire at any time. But I've always known, deep down, that I want to continue working. I just never knew why. I love solving problems, and work provided me with the opportunity to do that. It seems foolish to retire from something I love.

I've been told that working too hard burns you out. I've been told I'm money hungry or driven from pure vanity to achieve success, that I'm chasing an empty dream. Culturally, I was not taught to strive for the most life has to offer. I was told to work hard enough to make a good salary, buy a house, get married, and survive life as it is. That's a fulfilling life for some, but I always wanted something different. I would often dull my work ethic to meet the expectations of those around me.

In my mid-thirties, I began to embrace my own work ethic. I grew unafraid of how others perceived me, because of it. I woke up early in the morning and got a head start on the day. I wanted to work, to spend endless hours doing something I loved. My ambition matched my work ethic and the results were phenomenal. Because I didn't make a distinction between work and play, it spoke to me when 50 Cent said he loves work more than playing. The same passion I applied when I was a child playing soccer, building Legos, and making people laugh has now been applied to business strategy, marketing, and running a consultancy. I view work as play.

The idea that work and play should be distinct is outdated. It confines us to a world where you can have only a little at a time of both. The bit we want to get from play is usually happiness or fulfillment, so why should this not be possible at work?

Why does what we do for a living have to be something we despise? Why is anything not considered work more valuable? Work has been my vehicle to becoming a better person. By working, I learned the most important lessons in life, my greatest strengths, deepest fears and insecurities, my greatest highs and lowest lows. It doesn't matter what task I am working on or what industry I am in. Work gives me a sense of purpose and fulfillment. It has always been a channel for learning about life. That's what drives me to continue investing time and energy into work.

People say that if you do for a living that which you love, you never work a day in your life. Even the Bible describes work as something essential to life, something that ascribes meaning. How about investing your time in activities that not only ignite your sense of vitality but also contribute positively to the world? The existence of separate work and play entities only allows you to experience happiness and fulfillment from either in fragmented moments. My favorite life lesson about work and play is that they're one and the same.

54

Uncertainty is where things happen.
Uncertainty is where new happens.

—Gary John Bishop,
Unfu*k Yourself

Gary John Bishop explains in his book how our need for certainty evolved from avoiding dangers, such as getting eaten by wild animals, centuries ago. Today we understand this feeling as making sure to not say the wrong thing in a meeting, or the avoidance of trying new things out of fear of appearing foolish. I have always wanted to know the exact outcome of things in my life. In retrospect, it was fear of uncertainty that drove my actions.

You can live a fulfilling life chasing certainty. You hope to remain unscathed in your journey, but when the inevitable moment arrives that something doesn't go the way you expected, everything comes crashing down around you. In a sense, it's a double blow, because you realize that you might as well have taken a chance on the uncertain, since obviously, there is no certainty in life.

Jim Rohn, American entrepreneur and writer, reminds us that risk is inherent in life. It's all risky. The moment you were born, life got risky; the moment you entered a relationship, it got risky; and just how risky, he asks? You'll end up dead; that's how risky life is.

My belief that I had substantial control over my life was an illusion I perpetuated in myself for a long time. It is in our nature to know this as well. When we make a decision, a gnawing feeling inside tells us we could have done more, could have chosen differently, yet we opted not to, for fear of the unknown.

Your personal pathway to opportunity lies in embracing uncertainty. It's the environment in which you grow, experience new things, and produce new, unprecedented results. Almost every time I have broken a glass ceiling in my life, it has come out of the necessity to take advantage of what I had in front of me, even the remnants of something that did not go as planned.

Mastering the art of becoming comfortable with uncertainty has been challenging for me. The only thing I'd improved at was recognizing my own fears of something going wrong. We have a wide range of possibilities at our disposal, if we are open to how they can manifest. This is not an excuse to live life recklessly or be devoid of direction, it's about aiming in the direction of your dreams, and not being tied to one path to get there.

Often, when I reflect on my own success, I don't regret reaching a certain milestone or ponder the unexpected steps that led me there; instead, I'm glad I went through it all. Embrace uncertainty, because when nothing is certain, anything is possible.

55

*My expectations were reduced to zero
when I was twenty-one. Everything from
then has been a bonus.*

—Stephen Hawking,
physicist, cosmologist

My life has been filled with unmet expectations that caused resentment toward people, places, or things around me. I had expectations for everything. There was a set of expected weather conditions, a set of anticipated traffic conditions, a set of expected reactions from my colleagues, and a set of expected behaviors from my wife, family, and friends. As I look back, I understand many of these expectations came from growing up in a community where so many shared the same values and lifestyle. I unintentionally adopted their measure for how things ought to be. That was how I experienced the world.

Unfortunately, it has the disadvantage of being a measure that is exclusively known by only me. I had now cast my life, my expectations, and my own personal reality on everyone and everything around me.

The truth became all too real when my wife and I went through the roughest time in our relationship. Through therapy I discovered that I had laid my unrealistic and mostly self-serving expectations over my wife, like a blanket. Every moment in my life was filtered through the prism of whether it met—or did not meet—my expectations.

Shakespeare said expectation is the root of all heartache. I didn't see my own behavior as the problem. I expected my wife to act in a certain manner in anticipation of my needs.

Hidden expectations accumulate over time and result in toxic negative perceptions of the world. It was only when my most precious relationship was on the brink of collapse that I was able to grasp the flaw in my worldview. Expecting that the world—or in this case, another person —will behave in a specific manner is unfair to them but also to you.

Living without expectations doesn't have to imply living a passive life, no longer setting goals. Remove your attachment to your expectations. When something inevitably doesn't go according to plan, you can move forward unshackled by those expectations.

Expecting that life should be a certain way is lazy. It's lazy to blame others, never taking responsibility for how your actions and thoughts reinforce your perception that life isn't going as planned. When you put your expectations on someone else, it's a curse for you and a curse for the person you expect to live up to the vague and unannounced specific action you predetermine in your mind.

Embracing reality empowers you to deal with life's unpredictable nature rather than being filled with resentment and self-pity about how things didn't work out. Release your expectations, and alleviate the obligation to fulfill them that you place on the world.

56

*If you want to improve, be content
to be thought foolish and stupid.*

—Epictetus,
Greek philosopher

When I first started working out, I focused on following the movements that my brother and friends taught me. I was not working out for the true benefits. Rather I was trying to not look foolish.

Despite not thinking much about it at the time, this type of behavior influenced my life in several ways. The reason I wouldn't do or try something new was because I'd embarrass myself, or it was because other people were already so advanced. The gap was too wide for me to catch up, so why even bother? I was apprehensive about learning something new or developing a skill, even when I really wanted to learn.

My best friend advised me to try something new one day. It's called CrossFit. True fitness enthusiasts often ridicule CrossFit, because of its seemingly dangerous workouts, the way it raises your heart rate and the lack of discipline in its movements. What I remember most vividly about my experience was that on day one, the coaches told me to begin with why I was there to develop good practices. This caught me completely off guard. I had thought we'd immediately begin working on a barbell or flipping a 500-pound tire.

It was inspiring to discover that others felt the way I had at various points in my life. We were now given

111

the opportunity to create lasting change. CrossFit is more about being part of a community that encourages personal growth than it is about the workouts themselves. The pursuit of improvement isn't to be feared; it's to be embraced. The push to improve unlocks something within us. The workouts themselves were merely the vehicle through which we spent hours upon hours improving ourselves.

Doing things we're afraid of is exactly what we need to break free from any mold that currently enslaves us. It turned out that where I would stop in CrossFit was also exactly where I would stop in other parts of my life. CrossFit became my daily medicine. I would attempt a one-rep max power clean every day. In that mere attempt, I gained the confidence to confront other difficult situations in my life. The positive changes I saw on the other side more than made up for the difficulties of enduring to gain a lasting positive change. Looking foolish will always be temporary. A bad day for the ego, they say, is a good day for the soul.

When you're young, you're taught to fear being considered foolish. It is the very thing that casts you as an outsider in a community. Many times, it is really only ourselves that believe others are laughing at us. I often made up stories for myself about why someone was staring at me. I believed I was being judged, but there really is no way to know if you're being judged. Your inner voice is just telling you, you're a fool.

The truth is, you're not that important to most people. I literally broke bones doing CrossFit, and the biggest mockery I ever felt came from within me. Fear of looking foolish is mostly a result of imagined anxieties about real problems, where the failure that comes with improvement might be worse than the consequences of not even trying. If you want to improve, be content to be thought of as foolish. Then you'll always receive the amazing gift of personal growth in return.

57

When you get it,
reach back, pull someone else up.

—Denzel Washington,
American actor

It wasn't until I was well into my twenties that I learned this lesson. As the youngest of three, I learned I could get whatever I wanted. Because I didn't have a younger sibling, I thought the treasures ended with me. Once I'd gotten what I wanted, why would I need to pass it on? For most of my life, I was blind to the multitude of people who took care of my needs, helped me along my path, and paved a well-worn road where I could easily navigate life. It's easy to overlook the people who shape the environment in which you thrive.

All of your parents, siblings, mentors, friends, and one-time acquaintances played a crucial role in equipping you for success. Denzel Washington reminds us not to aspire merely to make a living, but to aspire to make a difference. Our childhood years are spent learning the importance of working hard and achieving our goals. I never fully understood the importance of helping those around me succeed as well. My old attitude was, if I gave up my secret recipe, I would lose my competitive edge.

Helping someone brings them closer to their dreams, but what does that do for mine? For many years (though it's shameful to admit), looking out only for myself was just the way I lived. When all the things you wanted in life have been realized, you'll feel a shallowness, an emptiness that I liken to eating your favorite meal but finding it has no taste. Success experienced alone is unfulfilling. I've come to realize the greatest fulfillment is in helping others realize their potential.

Using your inherent skills is a moral obligation you have to the world. I've had many successes where others helped me to get where I am. I never took a moment to think about those coming up behind me and ask whether they needed assistance.

Being helpful to others and helping others achieve their dreams fosters reciprocity. It's what gives our lives a larger sense of purpose. Yes, continue to strive for success, but keep in mind the possibility that it could benefit someone else. This is a key component to ensure your efforts will benefit others.

When people are in their fifties, often, they begin to realize that no matter what success they have, it will be only their success if they don't leave a legacy. What would your legacy be? What do you want to be remembered by?

Denzel says, you never see a U-Haul following a hearse. I love that sentiment, because it reveals the dual-edged sword of spending an entire life chasing personal success, only to celebrate that success...by yourself. Your impact on the world is truly measured by the people you help along the way. You'll be remembered for the impact you have on others, not for having money, titles, homes, or cars. It can start a chain reaction of lifting others up that will last generations.

Being of service doesn't mean just waiting for someone to ask for your help. When Johnny Cash was dying, he emphasized that all he wanted to do was to give away all that he had built by himself, which he viewed as nothing more than dirt. His was a cold, practical calculation that, when we look back on our lives, we may have achieved great things, but that success is meaningless if we didn't also lift up our larger community.

58

*Work harder on yourself
than you do on your job.*

—Jim Rohn,
American entrepreneur, writer

For so long, I tried to make as much money as possible. As a fifteen-year-old, I worked at an amusement park. I was paid roughly $4.00 an hour to clean strollers. I didn't have the sense to avoid asking other people how much they made, nor did my friends keep it secret. Finding out that someone made more than I did discouraged me. Surely the person who made $5.00 was more valuable than I was.

I became fixated on the idea that what I made was never enough, that those who made more were somehow more valuable than I was, and that somehow that made me worthless. For each role that I took, I tried to make as much money as I could. When I finally got my first salaried job, I thought I'd made it. I realized that even if I were paid more, a sixty-hour work week would cut my earnings by 30 percent. I continued to experience a treadmill of financial aspirations into my late thirties. It wasn't until I came across this idea that everything changed.

To work on yourself more than on your job may seem counter-intuitive to the project of success. But it was only when I began working on myself—to enhance my skills in public speaking, acquiring a deep understanding of data and analytics, or acing project management—that my pay began to rise. I was adding more value to the workplace. People would hear about a well-done task, which would prompt an inquiry for some assistance, then another. Within a few years of investing in my skills, I had nearly doubled my income. The skills I'd developed had demonstrated my value to leadership.

People will pay for your ability to solve a problem or bring those solutions to others. Everyone has problems. If you're able to solve a problem for them, they'll pay you generously for your services. My decisions to work harder on certain skills came from simply talking to people who needed solutions. When a skill was lacking, I saw it as an opportunity to capture market share. I released my past negative belief that money demonstrated my value as an individual. The money I make now reflects the value I add to my marketplace.

For the record, every marketplace is different, but your level of self-development usually corresponds directly to the value your marketplace offers. The beauty of this concept is that it works like compound interest: it will increases over time as you continue to invest in your skills.

The pursuit of success is often confused with the pursuit of money. When you strive for the highest level of excellence, you will achieve sustainable success, and yes, you will be well compensated for your effort. Employers understand when an employee is seeking money or when they're offering value. The search for money is not only self-serving and limiting, it also impedes your ability to focus on the one thing you should be doing, which is investing in your skills to add value in the marketplace.

59

*Most people want to get what they want,
whereas the secret is to want what you get
at this moment.*

—Eckhart Tolle,
author, spiritual teacher

I have built a lasting relationship with expectations from people, places, objects, or events. My thinking was two-fold: In order to be fulfilled, I need expectations, and they need to be exactly what I want them to be. I had no interest in wanting only what I got at any given moment. Clearly, I deserved everything my heart desired and everything my mind could conjure, because I was a good person.

I set an expectation: if I was a certain way or did a certain thing, the world would reciprocate in exactly that same way, or ideally, a little more. The problem here: no one owes you anything. Here's the hard truth: not even those closest to you owe you anything.

Assuming others will do something that specifically meets your exact needs is like expecting them to find their way out of a maze, blindfolded and without any ability to hear or touch. I rarely give my children what they desire, though I always provide them with what they require. Yet, I would hate a world that treated me that way.

My demands were clear. I wanted my way. Now. As cringeworthy as it sounds, I don't believe I'm the only person who experiences this. There are nevertheless better and more effective ways to deal with your feelings when your expectations are not met. If you expect nothing from others, it doesn't mean you're becoming reckless about how the world treats you. It's the greatest gift you can give to someone to allow them to be exactly who they are in the world, and reciprocate as they best see fit.

The reality is, the people who are closest to you do their best to provide you with what you need—as they see it, through the lens of their own perspective. It might seem ideal if they reciprocated in the exact way you'd like them to, but you can't count on that to happen. By accepting people, places, objects, or events as they are, we accept life and fully embrace the present moment. To do this, you have let go of what you believe your life should be and commit yourself to work with the circumstances you are in.

I love the scripture "work your land," because what else can one do? Though I may wish things had turned out differently in my life, things really are unfolding precisely as they should. Most of us are likely to experience some form of disappointment from the world. The world is going about its business, but you are the one assigning meaning to everything.

"Life is very good if you ask nothing, expect nothing, and accept everything," says actor Sir Anthony Hopkins. There is nothing wrong with aspiring to a bright future and setting ambitious goals; after all, we all need direction and purpose in our lives. However, when you set expectations, you've created an absurd framework that no individual, thing, place, or event will be able to meet. Effectively, you're telling life you're only up for playing if it's by your rules. In that case, no one wins.

60

If you don't break your ego,
life will break it for you.

—Jay Shetty,
Think Like a Monk

For someone who loved to look good, I was unaware that I had an ego. For years. In my mid-thirties, someone happened to mention I was only 5' 7", but with my ego I stood 6' 1". This was a joke among my coworkers. They told anecdotes confirming my out-of-control ego. What's worse, they viewed it as an inherent trait that they'd come to accept, even welcome, because they'd only ever seen me as such.

My humiliation came from the fact that I knew, deep down, it was true. I laughed it off as if nothing had happened, but I had recognized this trait in myself for the first time. In that moment, I could hear my ego yelling at me to do something about this, don't let them belittle you, you're the best, they can't compare to you. My ego was on fire. I could feel it burning inside of me. It felt as if I were locked in a cage with the ugliest side of myself and couldn't escape.

For years I'd ridden a wave of self-esteem, and I'd never known any other way of life. I was 100 percent confident at all times, had received public recognition, awards, accolades, and perks. At the time of my height incident, I realized that the extent of what I'd achieved or taken credit for would actually fill many lifetimes. Being humbled was one of the most beneficial experiences in my life. I was reminded of my egocentric nature—not necessarily to be the best, but to be viewed as the best.

One of the best things about Jay Shetty's book is drawn from his time as a monk, the relationship between ego and humility. Two things should be remembered and two forgotten. It's important to remember both the bad we've done to others and the good others have done for us. The bad we've done to others reminds us of our shortcomings and keeps us grounded. The good others have done for us allows us to be humbled and grateful. The two things to forget are the good we've done for others and the bad others have done to us. As a reminder to not be overly impressed with yourself, forget about the good you've done for others. To no longer be focused on yourself, to release your feelings of anger, hate, or sadness, forget the bad that others have done to you.

The ego hates this matrix, because it doesn't have room to flourish. When I feel my self-importance rising, these four things keep me humble. They serve as a constant reminder that I am not that important. The point is not to come off as self-deprecating, but to keep my ego in check so that I can be more useful to this world instead of being a constant taker, which was my ethos for years.

The example of salt, which Shetty mentions in his book, also reinforces humility. No one ever notices when salt is added to a dish perfectly. When it is lacking or excessive, it is blamed. There's nothing wrong with being quite useful to the world without receiving credit for it. Starving the ego will always feed the soul.

61

If you want a new outcome, you will have to break the habit of being yourself and reinvent a new self.

—Joe Dispenza,
scientist, teacher, and lecturer

Most people I know long for change in their life. Like myself, many of them are afraid of the unknown that comes with change and with letting go of what is familiar. Joe Dispenza shows us how we continue to repeat patterns for years, not necessarily because they're beneficial for us, but because they're familiar to us. It's natural for us to gravitate toward what is familiar, even if it's painful, because historically it has been known to us as bearable.

The familiar can be anything in life—unhealthy eating habits, unfulfilling jobs, even abusive relationships. We all experience some discomfort when stepping into the unknown or breaking old habits. Knowing there is no end date for the discomfort you will feel may be frightening, but it's the very essence of that moment. You've entered the river of change.

My change was the reinvention of my persona. I was known for being funny, carefree, and lighthearted when I was growing up. It helped me become accepted socially, to meet girls, and to thrive. I began to realize these attributes had not served me well when I was a new husband, wanting to get serious about my career and start a family.

In the early stages of my life I realized that people expected me to behave in particular ways. When I didn't meet those expectations, I felt hated and abandoned. I hold no grudges against those who anticipated these aspects of me. It was difficult, at that time, to articulate that I was in the midst of change and needed support. Not until I had discarded my old self did I realize I was discarding something others had come to know and love. Could I really blame them for being upset?

It was hard to maintain the course when I noticed people around me suffering, because I seemed to be transforming into someone else. The persona or character that I'd created in my early years had flourished, but it was time to reinvent myself. I needed to create someone better suited to handle my new goals and aspirations.

I didn't know which was scarier, discarding my old self or knowing that I could so quickly create a new me. I've realized that we all play characters in life, generating personas to help us thrive.

American actor and artist Jim Carrey once said that depression is an indicator that deep down inside, you no longer want to play the character you created. Many people believe we're born with fixed traits, but we can be whoever we decide to be. What we're accustomed to thinking is wrong. Persona is not inherent; it is malleable. The uncomfortable experiences you encounter when you reinvent yourself may be frightening, yes, but they're no more frightening than remaining the exact same.

62

Nothing has a stronger influence psychologically on their environment and especially on their children than the unlived life of the parent.

—Carl Jung,
Swiss psychiatrist

Your child's potential becomes evident when you see the glimmers of natural talent and inherent strength they possess. My daughter at age five is very well-spoken and explains clearly what she wants, whereas my son has high emotional intelligence and easily engages with others. I was in my twenties before I realized the importance of these skills. When I look at my kids, I wonder what they may be capable of when they are my age if they develop these skills now.

Due to my own unfulfilled potential, I find myself wanting to nurture their gifts, even thought they didn't ask me to. It's somewhat embarrassing to be jealous of your own kids. I identify with this quote from Carl Jung, because until I had kids, I didn't realize I could have done more with my own life.

It's been said that children change your life, but I'd never grasped that they could also inspire you to change your own. In many ways, a child's new life represents a second chance. It was difficult for me be unselfish, to guide their lives in a way that would make up for my own past regrets and shortcomings.

I had a regimented life as a child. My first eighteen years were already planned out for me: what schools to attend, which friends to have, what foods to eat, what hobbies to take up, and even what clothes to wear. I was never asked what skills or talents I wanted to develop. This engendered, through conformity, a sense of defiance.

Actor Kevin Hart once said the only thing he spoils his kids with is the opportunity to try new things, things that stimulate their interest, watching to see what resonates with them. I love the notion that parents can have guiding principles for our children to use as north stars, but more importantly, to introduce them early to the power of choice. I hope to give my kids the freedom to choose the lives that inspire them with purpose and joy.

At those times I was most adamant that they pursue a certain activity, I never asked or considered whether it was what they wanted. On occasion, I found myself reinforcing stereotypes of male and female attitudes and behavior. Although I don't believe a five-year-old is capable of making a career choice, children do possess the ability to judge whether or not they're interested in a particular activity. The unlived life of a parent is regret, disguised so as to make them believe they're doing what's best for their children. The ability to guide and support someone's growth, done impartially and without impressing your own beliefs, will be one of the best second chances you'll get in your unlived life.

63

You get in life
what you have the courage to ask for.

—Oprah Winfrey,
talk show host, producer

Asking for what you want sounds easy enough. It's certainly simple to promote to others, but when I wanted something, I never had the courage to ask for it. I've associated asking for something with self-centeredness.

I grew up in a traditional immigrant family, where the only kind of work was hard work. You must always be grateful for what you have, and what you have is all you need. These are great ideas when it comes to basic survival requirements such as food and shelter, but what about deeper desires and aspirations? I always felt the line was blurry at that point, though I never knew if it was okay to request anything. Other people asked, and seemed to get what they wanted. Still, it seemed out of reach to me. I would sometimes tell myself that I wasn't deserving. Who was I to ask? I developed a correlation between asking for something and deep feelings of embarrassment and unworthiness.

As I grew up, my reticence turned to anger. I kept seeing things I wanted and yet never asked for them. I was angry at myself in two ways. First, I knew I could get what I wanted. I could have asked for anything from material possessions such as toys or clothes to something as personal as love and affection. Second, lacking the courage to ask resurrected my feelings of guilt, embarrassment, and unworthiness.

Oprah specifically uses the word "courage" in this quote, because so many of us grew up wanting things, but only a few of us had the courage to ask for them, because asking for something creates internal conflict. As I've matured, I've realized the internal conflict comes, not from wanting material things, but from the actions. My bad habit of believing my behavior toward a certain outcome was also making it clear what I wanted. It was easier to not ask and just hint at what I wanted.

When I wanted a promotion, I'd work harder at my job and only hint that I wanted a promotion. When I was passed over, it only strengthened the inner voice that told me I should be content with what I had. I wasn't worthy. I didn't deserve it.

Expecting others to know what you want isn't reasonable. Getting upset when your desires are unfulfilled is unfair to both you and others. Be specific. Know what you want and be courageous asking for it. Most of us don't want our significant others to just show affection. We want a hug or a kiss or to make love. No one knows what you want. It's up to you to make known that which you desire.

If you want a promotion, ask for it. If you want affection, ask for it. If you want help doing the dishes, ask for it. Most of the time, other people don't object to your desires. Most will do what they can to fulfill them. Giving to others actually brings us just as much joy as receiving something we want. Don't deny others the opportunity to give.

Asking for what you want is important, but being thankful for what you receive is also crucial. The moment you ask for something is the exact time to let go of your expectations for how it will come to pass. The act of asking is very fulfilling. Living in the safety of never asking for what you want is the surest way of never receiving what you desire.

64

Knowledge works. It builds up, like compound interest. All of you can do it, but I guarantee not many of you will do it.

—Warren Buffett,
American businessman

I didn't realize, growing up that I didn't value education. I had always enjoyed going to school, because I was able to hang out with my friends and make others laugh. Learning was just a necessary formality I had to deal with in order to have fun. That I ended up at a community college without any direction at a time when my friends were attending universities wasn't a surprise to me. I'd wasted twelve years of top-tier private schooling, and I was also lost in a new environment without friends to play or laugh with. I wondered why people didn't want to have fun all day or why people attending community college were spending their time studying.

When I had to do critical thinking or put together an essay, my work was mediocre. Then, I decided to double down on my physical skills, abandoning my feeble attempts to learn, to work in a trade. I became a chef in eight years, but I remained at the same level, even with many years of experience, with no real advancement. I could cook a mean osso bucco, but I could barely think critically, write effectively, or articulate my thoughts.

After meeting my wife, I realized I needed to make more money than my restaurant career was offering. I needed new skills. Potential employers, outside of restaurateurs, had little to no interest in hiring me. When I got a job in corporate food service—to help create a healthy food program for Genentech—it was pure luck. Several years later, I found myself in the same position: eager to grow. But without a real foundation, or more years of experience, I was beyond frustrated. It was depressing.

It has been said, rock bottom is a great foundation on which to build. I took one online course, and everything changed. In addition to reading and writing again, I had to articulate my own ideas and understandings of concepts in order to progress. There was no easy way out.

After four years of accelerated courses, I completed my bachelor's and master's degrees. I like to think that I made up for all those lost years in the classroom.

Looking at it through a financial perspective, I made $23,000 at age eighteen, $50,000 at twenty-six, and $90,000 at thirty-two. When I realized four years later that learning is important, I nearly quadrupled my income to $350,000.

This is only one example of how the thirst for knowledge affected my life. I developed a new perspective and the discipline to perform quality work, to see projects through with excellence, to be timely, articulate, and a better writer, essentially all things my peers had learned nearly twenty years previous.

It was as if Warren Buffett was talking about me when he said "most don't do it." I didn't take knowledge seriously and it hurt me. I think the quote "how you do anything is how you do everything" should be bolted on every classroom door. It took me twenty years to figure it out. I know there are lots of people out there who, like me, figure it out late.

Take learning seriously, period. Knowledge will always be the key to adding value to the world. As you gain new skills and insights, you're able not only to improve the quality of your own life, but to bring benefit to your community. This is the surest way to develop your unexpressed potential.

65

Your outcomes are a lagging measure of your habits.

—James Clear,
Atomic Habits

I never saw habit as a driver of my achievements. They were simply my personality. I thought if I achieved something, it'd be the result of a single action. If I didn't take that singular action, nothing would change.

Clear's book changed my mind. It broadened my perspective and taught me that everything I achieved or received has been manifesting for years in tiny behaviors. I didn't bother learning new skills, because I didn't earn what I wanted. When my health was poor, I ate fast food and often drank alcohol. I didn't consider that these small habits were the actions that made me broke and unhealthy.

Humans evolved to prioritize immediate rewards over delayed ones, Clear writes. As the youngest of three, I grew up accustomed to immediate rewards. What is immediately rewarded is repeated and what is immediately punished is avoided. Clear's ideas helped me realize why I preferred eating a cheeseburger to a salad. The consumption of one cheeseburger doesn't make me overweight, but the satisfaction I receive is instantaneous. In contrast, eating a salad doesn't immediately result in great health, and it also doesn't provide me with any satisfaction.

129

I looked at delayed gratification as the denial of well-deserved fun or enjoyment. Clear writes that every action is a vote for who you wish to become. This really struck me. I began looking at my daily actions through this lens. I found I was receiving tons of immediate rewards, but creating little to no long-term value. Because small changes don't seem to matter very much at the moment we're doing them, we ignore them. This is how I ended up with high cholesterol and no retirement savings at the age of twenty-eight.

Clear teaches how to improve our desired outcomes by developing systems to maintain and implement small "atomic" habits. A single implementation won't make a difference, but the compounding effect of dozens of small daily habits changes your life trajectory. Just like a plane, if you veer off course just a few degrees, you may end up in a different state.

The most valuable system for creating a lasting habit for me was joining a culture where my desired behavior was the norm. When I began to interact with other fitness enthusiasts I discovered better nutrition and longer-lasting routines. The secret to success is not just the setting of goals, but building a system that supports our tiny new habits to flourish. It's one thing to say you wants this, Clear tells us. It's something very different to say you are this. When you build the tiny habits that enhance your life, not only will your circumstances improve, but who you are as a person—your very identity—will be shaped as well.

66

*I have never let my schooling
interfere with my education.*

—Mark Twain,
American writer, philosopher

While I was completing my MBA, I thought what I learned would be applicable solely to my work. It would provide me with added value in the marketplace. I expected I'd have days when I wouldn't feel like completing the program, so I paid the entire tuition in advance.

Even on the toughest days when I had multiple assignments piling up, my full-time job required travel, my consultancy demanded more of my time, I had a weightlifting competition on the horizon, and my wife and kids wanted quality family time, I not only managed to handle it all but thrived in the thick of it.

To conquer an island, a famous conqueror once said, you must burn your boats. The moment you have no way out, something miraculous happens. It became clear to me that there is someone in me who is not only willing but is capable of adapting to my new environment. The construct of time became something I could wield instead of something that controlled me. When everything mattered to me, I become extremely resourceful. I awakened to a new part of myself that broke my previous restraints in ways I couldn't have imagined.

My schooling was never an interruption to my education; it was the vessel that revealed my higher self to me. I learned I was capable of accomplishing difficult things, even when I lacked motivation. I learned new concepts and applied principles that shook my beliefs to the core, and I developed enough humility to ask for assistance when I needed it. Working hard is difficult, and often just sucks!

When you haven't reached your full potential, you know you haven't fully tapped into your capabilities. The seeds of guilt and regret are planted and can corrode the will to live. Be inspired by the snowball effect: doing the hard things, even when you don't want to, builds character and makes other life challenges easier. The tasks stay the same, but you change.

When there is no other way out, you can operate with a sense of purpose that you wouldn't normally have. Going through this struggle gave me way more confidence than I ever imagined. It gave me the satisfaction of knowing I could see something through. It substantially increased my ability to openly confront life's challenges. School was the environment that afforded me the gift of learning about my truest self. How you do one thing is the way you do everything, so when something pushes you, don't run from it, push back. You may be pleasantly surprised with the person you encounter on the other side.

67

The magic thing about home is that it feels good to leave, and it feels even better to come back.

—Wendy Wunder,
The Probability of Miracles

When I moved out of my parents' home, I was ecstatic to finally have a place to lay my head at night that wasn't under their roof. It represented independence and the start of a new life. Unbeknownst to me, I was leaving behind a deep sense of certainty. I grew up with abundance. Things were always available to me, whether it was food, education, entertainment, or —particularly—love.

When I became a father, I discovered this lack of certainty. As I began the journey of fatherhood, I began to lose my grip on myself. I didn't know any more if I was a great husband, if I could still identify as a brother and son, or even if I could call myself a good friend. I never understood why I was unable to appreciate what was in front of me, the incredible waterfall of abundance flowing through my life. I couldn't understand where my anxiety was coming from.

My need for certainty correlated with my longing to find the peace of mind and assurance I had growing up. My thoughts kept returning to a notion that I would turn a corner, and suddenly there would be my certainty. There would be a plan telling me how to go about what

I needed to do. I didn't know if I could be the person I finally had the opportunity to become.

It's easy to take for granted the elements that comprised your childhood environment without realizing they were meticulously planned and prepared by those who raised you. I've learned that it's only through diligent planning and execution that I'm able to create the type of life I want, or in this case, the type of home environment for which I now longed.

They say that there's no better feeling than seeing things finally fall into place when you've seen them fall apart for so long. Through my internal struggle it became clear that only by meticulous planning would I be able to experience the same feelings of certainty and warmth I remembered growing up. When I began to act on this insight, a sense of certainty did begin to reappear, and the wonderful journey began once again.

With my wife and two children as my focus, I nurtured an environment where we were each free to create the world we wanted. Home is where creation begins. Home is where you bring your anxieties, fears, and worries to the table so you can work through them together with your family. Home is where you work on maintaining a focus on your vision.

Author and historian Edward Everett Hale wrote that coming together is a beginning, keeping together is progress, and working together is success. Working together as a family to create the life we all desired re-created the sense of certainty I'd been seeking. It had nothing to do with going home; it had to do with making a choice: to create the best life possible in the presence of those I most cherish.

68

Shame is the most powerful master emotion.
It's the fear that we're not good enough.

—Brené Brown,
The Power of Vulnerability

I don't know many people in life who haven't experienced feeling inadequate. It certainly was a feeling I had in my childhood. Not that my parents were promoting my inadequacies, but rather, my self-comparison to older siblings combined with my treatment as the youngest made for a childhood filled with bullying.

Because I didn't fully understand how to defend myself, I became a punching bag for the majority of my early years. My story was that I wasn't good enough. I reinforced this daily by actively looking for the ways my siblings were better than I. It was effortless, just because they were older. They already had a variety of accomplishments under their belts. Inadequacy wasn't just something I felt. I thought I was born that way.

Brené Brown explains the difference between guilt and shame. Guilt says, I did something wrong. Shame says, I am wrong. When we feel guilt, we want to share with others, but shame makes us want to hide from others. That I felt I wasn't good enough wasn't the issue. The real issue was feeling ashamed about not being good enough.

Brown says that shame damages the very part of us that believes we are capable of change, something that resonated with me deeply. Shame requires three things to flourish in our lives: secrecy, silence, and judgment. This potent trio struck me when I first learned about it, and even more when I realized it was my drug of choice. It was the perfect cocktail for growing up unconfident and resentful.

I'm not angry that it took me well into my thirties before I truly understood this concept. I've come to realize that fear of not being good enough never truly leaves a person. It takes practice to recognize that you're telling yourself a story. Many days, I still don't feel good enough. Sometimes as a father, sometimes as a husband, and many times as a brother, son, or friend. If I believe that I don't measure up, I am closing myself off from opportunities. The surest way to never experience something is to not attempt it.

Today I will attempt anything; anything that won't kill me. It's my way of making up for all the times I didn't do or say something I deserved to do or say. Brown taught me it's empowering to think of shame as a little gremlin that comes out only in the darkest of times and, just like in the movie, dies in the light. The shame I felt arose from my belief that I was born inadequate. This was the personal hell I created for myself.

The only one telling you you're not good enough is you. When you hide from the world, you're letting the walls of secrecy, silence, and judgment surround you, enclosing you in the prison of your mind.

69

Tomorrow becomes never.

—Tim Ferriss,
American inventor,
podcaster, speaker

As a lifelong procrastinator, I've mastered the art of Later. Later I'll have more energy. Tomorrow the weather will be better. Today I'm not motivated.

I once heard an idea that really resonated. The likelihood of feeling motivated at the exact moment you need to act is extremely unlikely. The ability to accomplish something regardless of how you feel is beautiful, because motivation is a fleeting emotion. No one feels bad about procrastinating for a day, but have you done it for years? I have. It's not a fun feeling but rather one of deep remorse that no one should experience.

In my early twenties, I completely stalled my personal development. I was married, I had a house, and I had a good job. Everything I had dreamed for my life had come true. I put off the day when I would become a better brother, son, and eventually, father. The day after tomorrow I would return to school, the day after that I would begin to exercise. My fear of tomorrow was at the heart of the matter. Despite what I'd already accomplished, I was afraid of doing something even bigger and failing.

Tim Ferriss says what we fear doing most is usually what we most need to do. Moreover, we tend to underestimate what we can do in a month, while overestimating what we're capable of doing in a day. Reading Ferriss, I realized that I was both deathly afraid of failing and impatient at the same time. I wanted things now, with the added benefit of assured success. "Doing it tomorrow" had ended up costing an additional ten years before I started to do the things I always wanted to do.

It was the birth of my children that helped change my perspective. Life is precious. The things I was doing for my family were not things I would do for myself. I regimented their nutrition, sleep, learning and development, as well as their environment. Yet I was complacent about these things for myself.

When my family's tomorrow became more important than my today, it made all these quotes hit home. My today actually ensures their better tomorrow. By setting out to do what I wanted to do, I got a double win. Typically, it resulted from accomplishing something I was passionate about that benefited my family in the process. By returning to school, I gained better skills, leading to an increase in my salary and position. I was able to eat better, get better sleep, and be more present and caring for my family when I was in good shape. The audiobooks I listened to helped me gain perspective, new skills, and insights that I could use to benefit my community.

We live in an eternal present. Tomorrow never actually arrives. The fear of failing is still very much in me, and my impatience hasn't changed. I've just decided that when I do feel these things, they don't have to be the reason my life doesn't happen.

70

F-E-A-R has two meanings: Forget Everything and Run or Face Everything and Rise. The choice is yours.

—Zig Ziglar,
American entrepreneur

Life is suffering. I remember first hearing this from Jordan Peterson, Canadian psychologist and author, and thought it was such a terrible notion, but the more I listened the more it resonated. Peterson noted that most major religions are centered around life being difficult. Not so much, because it's difficult and pointless, but that in order to succeed in this life, you have to be able to find meaning and purpose in what you do every day.

"Forget everything and run" has been my self-defense mechanism. It reinforced my feeling that avoidance was a positive thing. I would look at the potential dangers of a situation and prepare myself for the worst. By thinking ahead a few steps, I would ensure I could run out of harm's way. Selfish? I know, but the idea of facing everything and rising to meet it didn't appeal to me. Facing things seemed to constitute an acceptance of the notion that life is a struggle. It seemed wiser to focus on self-preservation.

It seems to me that one can certainly avoid pain in life, but in so doing, will avoid pleasure as well. The greatest things in life are on the other side of fear. Since my mid-thirties, I've adopted the practice of facing things and rising to the occasion. It has become the bedrock for some of the most positive changes in my life.

You are unlikely to attain something you desire without some degree of difficulty, but most people stop at those difficulties. Many factors could be contributing to this, but for me, fear was the most common reason. Fear of failure and embarrassment. It is at that exact moment, however, that you should double down on your commitment. Fear and embarrassment are signs that something great is just around the corner.

In challenging situations, fear manifests for me as failure, embarrassment, and a feeling of worthlessness. Who am I to think that I deserve what I want? The self-defeating talk I gave myself would actually enhance my anxiety.

It is impossible to know if you will succeed in all your life's ambitions, but one sure way you won't is by surrendering to fear. As Jim Carrey said, you can easily fail at something you don't enjoy, so you might as well take a chance on doing what you love. "Face everything and rise" is a motto I live by and an incantation I repeat frequently to remind myself: if I must suffer, then better to suffer in pursuit of something meaningful.

71

Learning a [skateboard] trick is kind of like a puzzle; you have to keep trying, and trying, and trying, and adapting and changing, and adapting and changing, and finally it works.

—Rob Dyrdek,
entrepreneur, pro-skateboarder

I only knew Rob Dyrdek as the skateboard guy on MTV's *Rob & Big*, but one day I came across an interview with Dyrdek and Tom Bilyeu. It blew my mind. I was astounded by Dyrdek's view of the world and by how he made skateboarding his medium of success, gaining upward of $100 million in total wealth.

It wasn't only his earnings that caught my attention. His simple philosophies on life also spoke to me. Adapting and changing constantly in order to learn a new skateboard trick can provide valuable insight into the process of achievement. Each iteration of the trick comes with its own unique challenge. With every adaptation you must maintain the same level of curiosity and passion as you had in the first attempt. To finally see it come to fruition is reassuring.

The challenge itself offers insight, and a measure of just how hard you need to work. The level of difficulty you experience must be met with the same—if not greater —level of passion. The key to making a fantasy come true, as Drydek did, is to try things. Hence the name of his popular TV show, *The Fantasy Factory*. He believed that when you make yourself a reality, everything in life becomes a fantasy.

My life had been filled with infinite fantasies that were only met with subpar efforts and feeble attempts. I had always tried things once, but rarely came back for a second dose of failure. I was the guy who boasted I had done everything. In reality, I'd only made attempts. I spent a lot of time fooling myself, even bragging that I had accomplished it all.

That's a small way to live your life. It's even worse when you look in the mirror and realize you're not winning, because you're unwilling to put in the work, believing your fantasy is simply not possible. I had many days where it seemed more convenient to ensure my dreams remained only fantasies, by executing a crappy attempt and then pretending to be surprised by the results.

Drydek also says, never undervalue the idea of partnership. You are the average of the five people you spend the most time with. Finding like-minded people requires an understanding of your strengths. Doing this was critical to my attempts to fulfill my dreams.

I've learned that accomplishment consists of three components. Initially, I see the challenge, then I begin to adapt and change, and finally, I rely on those around me, not necessarily to push me, but to remind me that the difficulties I encounter today are an important precursor to my fantasies becoming a reality.

72

*There is no coming to consciousness
without pain.*

—Carl Jung,
Swiss psychiatrist

Watching my wife face some of her challenges
has always inspired me. I tend to get defeated
easily. I run from pain. When I met my wife, I learned
a valuable lesson about resilience. Since we met, she's
seen all of her immediate family members pass away. I
assumed because no one was around anymore, living in
the house she'd grown up in would only foster pain and
sadness. I said we should move, and she asked why. Her
response changed everything for me. She said, although
it did make her sad, it also held memories of happiness
and joy.

I am the first to avoid pain, but she was willing to sit
through it and deal with the emotions. Her ability to meet
adversity head-on, without backing down, is something
I find most attractive. It doesn't matter whether her
opposition actually results in success.

My wife has rare qualities that can be emulated by
my children. Watching her overcome these challenges
provides me with the clarity that life always tests us.
Continuing to move forward and making the best of life
regardless of circumstances breeds uncommon character.
She views the world differently than most people do. I

believe that has also contributed to the evolution of our consciousness toward the challenges of life.

When I watch another person's struggles, I feel gratitude for what I have, and I understand that our evolution is dependent upon difficulties and struggles. I had also thought my wife's pain would subside at some point, but on many days it affects her as much as it did at the beginning. Yet she has exponentially increased her ability to deal with it.

Carl Jung calls consciousness the awareness that difficulties are part of life. He suggests we actively work through difficulties rather than run from them. In the end, not only is the process worth it, but it becomes a way of facing life's challenges head-on. Facing suffering, dealing with it, gives purpose to the pain. The definition of resilience is a capacity to recover quickly from difficulties. If you accept the pain, there will be something on the other side of that struggle. You will at the very least be a stronger, more resilient version of yourself. Sometimes, in dark places, we may believe we've been buried, when in reality, we have actually been planted.

73

*People are dream killers. You've got to be careful
who you give emotional access to.*

—Tyrese Gibson,
American actor, singer

The power of the quote above spoke to me on several levels. I'd always believed that if you truly want to accomplish your dreams, they must also be approved of and supported by the world. For example, when I started my career I wanted to be a chef. People told me I would make a great chef. I believed them. Having others believe in you is valuable, but I quickly embraced what others saw in me, because I didn't have a vision of my own. In fact, it was the decision to move away from cooking that caused others to question my motives.

After only a few years in the business, I aspired to take my career in a new direction. On TV one night, I saw an interview of Puff Daddy, the rapper. He said he had never wanted to be the on-stage guy. He wanted to be the guy making decisions on his cell phone backstage. This resonated, as I realized it was the same for me.

My goal was to be the person who owned the building and came up with the restaurant's concept, not to be the chef. I was in my early twenties and had no formal education (other than culinary school), so I had to start from scratch.

In the early 2000s, corporate dining was very different than it is now. At best, it was an adult lunchroom with mostly mediocre food and subpar service, both of which I wanted to oversee.

Now the questions and comments started rolling in. You don't want to be a chef anymore? Isn't it your dream to own your own restaurant? As a chef, I thought you were onto something.

During my worst days working in a corporate cafeteria, I was certain I'd made the biggest mistake of my life. But that was also when I realized, it's not someone else's responsibility to believe in my dream: it's mine and mine alone.

The more you pursue your dream without allowing others to dictate or even validate it, the clearer your dream becomes. Considering it was never my dream in the first place, I can't blame others for questioning it.

After pursuing my dream to run these cafeterias, to be the guy on the cell phone, I realized my strengths lay in communication and people skills. I moved into sales and marketing and am now the Vice President of Marketing for a multimillion-dollar VC-funded startup that is also a top 100 Y-Combinator company.

Tyrese says that when you change your mind it will change your life. If nothing around you changes, change the things that are around you. During my journey to become a vice president, I found that dream killers are those who have not detached from the group validation mindset.

They say it's not lonely at the top if you help someone else get there. This is the second component of the equation. Once you have identified your own dream, you must do what you can to help others identify theirs as well. Simply cutting out dream killers only directs their attention to someone else. There's nothing admirable about reaching the top and then pulling up the ladder behind you. I now thank those who questioned my dreams. Without them I wouldn't have asked myself the very questions that led me to realize my own dreams.

74

It's not luck, it's not magic, it's not circumstances. It's developing a great plan and executing on it, day in and day out until the visions in your head become your reality.

—Andy Frisella,
entrepreneur

When I became a vice president, I expected to feel different somehow. It had been on my list for years, even decades. It finally became a reality...with an underwhelming degree of normalcy. My pursuit required me to transform myself into that very thing, so achieving it felt somewhat like the process of pursuing it.

It became necessary to be extremely disciplined, not only at attending to work, but most importantly, remaining present. I took the time to understand the mission and vision of my company, even if it cut into other tasks. Rather than expecting something in return, I did what was best for the business. I assumed full responsibility and owned any shortcomings, not because of my team or my other department counterparts, but because of my own values. Communication could be improved. Preparation could be enhanced.

In less than four years, this mindset helped me quadruple my income and provided countless opportunities for career advancement. To achieve further advancement in my career, I realized I would have to first match my work ethic with my aspirations. This is what Andy Frisella talks about. It's not fun, it's not glamorous, and that feeling of success and happiness lasts for a few moments, at most. My title today represents a mental state and a larger purpose. My vision of becoming a vice president was nurtured through the long hours I put in, day in and day out. More importantly, it was nurtured by the long hours others invested in my success.

It would be easy to believe I'd made all this happen on my own, but it requires a village of people to clear the path for you. Every day represents a path to achievement. Financial and career growth are merely the side effects of a focus on something greater than yourself. Living purposefully is what was always missing from the equation of achievement for me.

Most people are capable of creating a vision for what their life should be like. If you're able to combine what motivates you with daily consistent effort toward that larger purpose, it becomes not just a formula, but the formula for success. It is a powerful ecosystem that enables you to succeed in life.

As Frisella tells it, he's simply an individual who makes a list of critical tasks to be completed every day and follows through on them. It's easy to think what differentiates one person from another, in terms of success, is inherent talent, allowing them to achieve success in a way most of us can't. It would be easy to believe that rather than simply putting in a daily effort, they possess God-given talent.

Use the word "grind" sparingly. It detracts from the meaning of daily work or service. Daily work reflects what you believe and what you hope to achieve in the world, as manifested through success and accomplishments along the way.

75

*Great ambition is the passion of great character.
Those endowed with it may perform very good
or very bad acts. All depends on the principles
which direct them.*

—Napoleon Bonaparte,
French emperor

I've always held great ambitions in life, wanting to reach the highest heights of what life offers. I remember being on a family vacation when my brother brought home a brochure for a 1997 Toyota Supra. In my mind, I vividly pictured what it would be like to drive this car, to have a successful career, and to come home to my beautiful wife in my big house. It wasn't as though I'd thought about it for only a few seconds. I admired the pictures and imagined my future for at least forty-five minutes. Even the ink on the brochure's pages smelled luxurious.

This moment was repeated hundreds—perhaps thousands—of times about various things in my life, things I knew I wanted to own. The more I imagined how my life would unfold, the less I did to make it happen. In the absence of a complementary work ethic, ambition is nothing.

Despite not owning that car today, I do come home to a beautiful wife, a large house, and have a successful career. For these things to be sustainable, ambition must not only match your work ethic but also be driven by your guiding principles. Only a few years ago, these things were either non-existent or hung by a thread.

Great ambition is like a laser. That laser can be applied with precision to assist in surgery, technology, and cutting and welding building materials. Lasers can also cause destruction, harm, or even death, when applied with malice.

My ambitions in life weren't consistent until I hit my mid-thirties. I know that ambition without a work ethic is useless, but ambition, without direction and guiding principles, is highly dangerous. My life has been filled with poor choices and behavior I am not proud of. In my worst moments, this was how I grew my career. Through ambition, I increased my knowledge of underhanded tactics and strategies. I did it to gain an edge over my competitors, to learn their weak points, in order to marginalize and bully them, and to adopt precise language to manipulate those I loved.

Certainly, ambition can lead to a successful relationship, a comfortable home, and a rewarding career, but just as important is how you got there. Imagine eating your favorite meal and tasting nothing. It brings a feeling of emptiness when you use ambition with self-serving principles. It is an offense against your very being. Having ambition is a gift, but it must be nurtured and cared for like a plant. Watering it with a strong sense of purpose and a solid moral compass allows you to narrow your attention to building instead of destroying.

When I began applying my ambition toward becoming a better husband, father, son, brother, and friend, everything changed. Giving instead of taking and developing an ambition that matched my work ethic were the necessary ingredients. They helped me heal a beautiful relationship, transform my family's house into a home, and evolve a career into something that serves a greater purpose. Ambition, work ethic, and guiding principles are the three elements required to manifest and sustain anything of value.

76

I love a success story, but even more than a success story; I like a dude who f*cks his life up and gets his life together again story.

—Joe Rogan,
American commentator, podcaster

This quote has a way of resonating with everyone. I believe it's not just about an underdog story, because we can all relate to it to some degree. Everyone has been there. At some point in our lives, we've all done something we thought was the end of the road, rock bottom. In that situation, it's liberating to know it can't get any worse.

There is something in each of us that lies dormant until a certain series of events unlocks it. For me, I knew that I'd hit rock bottom when I felt isolation. When I looked around and saw I was no longer surrounded by loved ones or those who had my best interest in mind. This was a guidepost, announcing I'd arrived at pure hell.

My true self was only revealed when I reached this point. It was the me that existed beneath layers of fear, anxiety, and self-doubt, a fragile person. This was when I knew I had to make a change.

To start with just you is a reset button. Begin by taking care of this fragile person inside of you. Acknowledge that your life is hanging by a thread. I found this motivating, because it gave me the opportunity to once again do something right, even if that was as simple as being kind to myself.

According to clinical psychologist Jordan Peterson, the moment of truth burns. Dead wood gets burned off. People don't like this, especially if they're already 95 percent dead wood. I found my real self in that 5 percent, and I didn't want to lose it. This is the exact approach to take when you can't help but fuck everything up. When you begin by caring for your most vulnerable self in a kinder, gentler, and more compassionate manner, you allow seeds to grow that can nurture this new self.

Rather than being proud of my accomplishments, I found myself compelled to make myself more useful to those around me. The guidance seemed to clarify what had previously been unclear, that I must shift my focus from inward to outward. My new path began to take shape when I made small steps toward becoming a better person. Once I'd hit rock bottom, journeying on that path felt uncomfortable and different. This was exactly why I needed to keep going. It was my path to redemption.

When I was rebuilding the person I am today, I felt like an imposter. I was playing a character, faking a better path for myself. Joe Rogan points out that far too often, we define ourselves by past failures. Those failures are not you. You're the person who learned from failure. Be comfortable with the fact that you'll not only reach rock bottom, but you'll experience an intense form of stress and struggle to create a new version of yourself. I'd never want to go back to rock bottom, but I'm sure that if I did, I'd look forward to meeting the new me that would emerge.

77

*The key to success is
to start before you are ready.*

—Marie Forleo,
author, TV host

When I first started my career, I'd heard that one should take a promotion, then figure it out from there. I couldn't grasp the idea of doing something before I was ready. When I was twenty-four, the wholesale bakery and cafe where I worked offered me a promotion, to run the whole operation. During my subsequent meeting with my boss, I vividly recall declining the offer with my head down. I could only see my inadequacies and focused on the problems I would surely encounter in trying to run a business I had little knowledge of. If so much pressure was placed on me, how could I possibly succeed at something that I'd never done before?

To this day, I regret having passed up that opportunity. I can't say my career trajectory was stunted as a result, but when I rejected the offer, it was as if I'd rejected my deepest desires. Telling someone who believed in me that I did not only made matters worse.

According to Marie Forleo, the only person who can make or break your dreams is you. I promised myself I'd never again doubt in my own capabilities. Nothing is worse than shouting to the world, "don't believe in me because I don't believe in myself!"

What we say to ourselves in the privacy of our own minds matters. Another quote by Forleo that I love is, everything is figure-out-able. When you believe in yourself and your abilities, you find a way to make it work. That's when something magical happens. When you begin a new endeavor, it's difficult to imagine success, because you have no benchmark for how you will handle it.

There's no way to predict your performance at a skill you have never attempted. You have to accept the fact that with growth comes unforeseen challenge.

Belief is the starting point for all of this. You become successful when you believe you'll succeed. Your level of resourcefulness kicks in and helps you navigate these new challenges. As you become more proficient at accomplishing difficult tasks, you become more innovative in your approach. You adapt your previous methods to new challenges.

There's no limit to what you can grow into. The mere fact that someone has done it before is proof it can be done. If no one has done it before you, just know there are millions of people who have also worked at learning how. Your feet begin moving in the direction of your dreams. With each awkward step along the way, you get better. The trick is to keep walking, and soon you will be running.

78

*Life contains but two tragedies. One is to not get
your heart's desires; the other is to get it.*

—Oscar Wilde,
poet and playwright

It took me years to realize the extent of my selfishness. As far as I could tell, people were out to get theirs, and theirs alone. I viewed it as an accomplishment to attain something for myself by any means necessary. It is rare for a great achievement to be celebrated in isolation, yet that is exactly what takes place when you are motivated purely by self-interest. The shorter the time it takes to satisfy a desire, the shorter the experience of value will be. My life was full of short moments.

Financially beneficial promotions degraded my character, because I had to deceive or manipulate in order to get them. My tendency to satisfy my immediate desires meant most of my decisions were hasty and benefited only me. When I finally accomplished something I'd been dreaming about, it left me with a sense of emptiness. The manner in which I'd achieved success just wasn't in line with how I'd envisioned it.

When you want something so badly you're willing to break rules, abandon commitments, lie, cheat, or steal, it is usually driven by a fleeting desire. Life's true treasures are rarely easily found. Attributes like hard work, discipline, and consistency are gateways to the fulfillment of your true desires. When something is obtained quickly without

155

much effort or intent, it doesn't allow you to enjoy it to the fullest. The road by which it was obtained dulls the pleasure.

I find myself going back to previous moments of unsatisfied fulfillment and wanting to re-experience them with a deep level of satisfaction in how they came to pass. I am, for example, no longer lazy with my wife. I don't try to show her how much I love her by lavish gifts or expensive vacations. Instead, I make her lunch, fold the laundry, and ask her how her day was, day after day. That's how I find the most precious moments of love, partnership, and gratitude. The joy is lasting, but so is the hard work required to maintain that deep fulfillment.

I heard a quote that speaks to my own far-too-frequent experience: In hell, you sit at a banquet with all your favorite foods, but you cannot taste anything, and you are driven by an endless appetite that can never be satisfied. Obtaining what you desire is very different from achieving what is truly satisfying and fulfilling to you.

79

Instead of wondering when your next vacation is, maybe you should set up a life you don't need to escape from.

—Seth Godin,
writer, marketing expert

I've always looked for greener pastures, never truly satisfied with what I had. Monday-through-Friday was not the real world; that was lived on Saturday and Sunday. Imagining what the future held was easier than putting in the work to make it a reality.

My favorite part of working at a job I hated was driving to work and daydreaming about the job I would one day have, or the fun I would have when I no longer worked at the current job. It was a daydream that lasted the full eight hours of my working day. That daydream was of living in a big house, achieving success in my career, and going on a dream vacation with my wife and children. Rather than simply daydreaming, I longed to do these things. This is a bad place to be, where you're no longer in the present. It's a diversion that only temporarily soothes the inevitable dissatisfaction that is brewing deep down. The problem is that it is easy to overlook this aspect of your life, as if turning off a part of you is somehow beneficial.

I hadn't realized I'd begun to live my life in only short bursts. For many years, I could remember only one or two moments from a 365-day year. Your entire lifetime will seem equivalent to maybe half a year when you multiply that out. It seemed far easier to live in a world

157

that allowed me to experience my dream life only once a year rather than striving to make my dreams reality.

As time progressed, I resented my own inaction about bringing my dream world into existence. Eventually, the line between reality and daydream became blurred. I began to believe I'd achieved that life. I forgot I was still working at a job I hated. I was no closer to being in a committed relationship. I wasted much of my twenties daydreaming my next vacation. It wasn't until I reached my mid-thirties that I was willing to set up a life that I wasn't vacationing from. It's a very difficult task.

An honest assessment of where you are relative to where you wish to be is both frightening and humbling. It may seem impossible to reach your desires, and worse, the road may not even be paved.

The reason vacations and daydreams had such allure was that, in my dream world, they were already accomplished. I didn't have to endure the hard work; I was already at the end of that. My imagination was too limited to fathom the satisfaction that comes with creating a life that's not lived only on weekends or vacation.

Having established a life there is no need to run from, you can finally see the greener grass, and it will always be much better than you imagined, because you'll actually be standing on it.

80

*Do more of what you love, less of what you
tolerate and none of what you hate.*

—John Assaraf,
writer, CEO and
cofounder of RE/MAX Indiana

A dear friend once told me, do what you love and
love what you do. This has become one of my
favorite quotes over the years. John Assaraf taught me the
second part. While doing what I loved always made me
feel alive, it was often diluted, because I did more of what
I loved only to balance out the things I merely tolerated
or even despised.

Distancing yourself from something you only tolerate
can be difficult. Distancing yourself from something you
hate is downright painful. I've done many things, because
I could tolerate being treated a certain way. I did them
because it was what I thought I should do.

In the early years of our lives, we are given as many
boundaries as possible, only to spend our later years
trying to break those boundaries. However, I believe this
is where the beauty of maturation resides. It's through
removing yourself from familiar constructs that you're
able to discover what makes you tick. These moments are
also sad, because you realize there are things in your life
you should give up, such as relationships, jobs, or even
the place where you live. The pain of removing things
you tolerate is necessary in order to clear the runway for
more of what you love to do.

When I made such changes, everything in my life began to revolve around what I loved doing. You'll find it easier and easier to tend the parts of your life that are the most meaningful to you. To pursue the things that make you come alive, identify and get rid of whatever doesn't support them.

I've come to appreciate the things I tolerated and disliked in my life. If not for those things, I probably wouldn't have found what I love. I used to hold resentment toward things I tolerated and hated, but now they're no longer part of my life I see them as the key ingredients of my current outlook. Assaraf says that most people are thinking about what they don't want, then wondering why it shows up over and over again. Through my own experiences, I now know that doing more of what I love entails the hardship of letting go.

81

If you want others to be happy, practice compassion. If you want to be happy, practice compassion.

—Dalai Lama,
spiritual leader of Tibet

The practice of compassion is considered by the Dalai Lama to be the ultimate expression of one's highest self. This quality is compelling, because it of its noble character. You hear about compassion as a trait consistent with great world leaders or as a quality of a selfless hero in a movie. There is a strong regard for compassion, because it requires doing something for another and expecting nothing in return.

Currently, we live in a society that emphasizes the importance of me-first values. A focus on the self entails withdrawing your gifts and talents from those who could benefit greatly from them. Performing random acts of kindness is not for the weak, but for those with a strong sense of moral obligation to better the world around them. They act to make a meaningful impact on the lives of others.

It is possible to light a thousand candles from a single candle so it never dims. I withheld my flame for many years, hoarding my gifts, skills, and talents for my own benefit. I've discovered the satisfaction that can be found only when practicing compassion toward others. That warm and fuzzy feeling is a sign that my soul is being nourished, that a layer is being peeled back to reveal my best self.

When you are acting out of compassion, you unlock the part of yourself that can also practice self-compassion. If your compassion doesn't include yourself, it's incomplete. We often fail to practice self-kindness. To grow personally and gain self-awareness, it is essential to be supportive and understanding toward ourself rather than being harshly critical. Self-compassion allows you to recognize stress without self-judgment.

When I make a mistake, I don't only judge myself. I harass, verbally abuse, and mock myself, using words I would never say even to my worst enemy. I've been guilty of verbally assaulting myself and have even caused myself physical harm, berating and condemning my own actions.

The most valuable lesson I learned from reading the Dalai Lama was to be kinder to others, because the kinder you are to others, the kinder you'll become toward yourself. To truly reach fulfillment, you must ensure that others can attain theirs.

82

Once children enter our life, their impact is indelible, and we are required to reinvent ourselves in response.

—Dr. Shefali Tsabary,
writer, coach

Until I became a father, I'd assumed I had a parenting template passed down to me by my parents. I thought I'd automatically be able to impart valuable lessons to my own children. They'd be the lessons I'd learned growing up. Those lessons would accelerate their success.

My experience as a relatively new father (six and four, as of this writing) has shown me the template mentality is both self-serving and selfish. Parenting was about me. I wanted to make the job of parenting just that: a job. A job where I would succeed. A job I would master, just like any new skill acquired at work.

Dr. Shefali taught me the importance of setting aside any sense of superiority in order to achieve a state of pure connection with your child. This seemed like such an odd notion to me. Children knew nothing, I thought, so how on earth could we be on a level playing field? What could they possibly teach me?

My connection to my own children ultimately came from identifying my own faults. This meant putting my own ego aside. Sure, my children are not familiar with marketing or finance, but they have an inherent sense of empathy and they are polite and know how to share. They're mindful, saying please and thank you at the appropriate moments. All of these are not strong characteristics of mine.

It upset me to learn that my kids possessed skills I had yet to master myself. It was a blow, but I realized I'd be able to create a deeper bond with them if I could both offer them lessons I've learned and be humble enough to learn from them.

By letting go of my sense of superiority, I've released my attachment to how things should be, surrendering to how things actually are. Despite how little they are, my children are already on their own paths. This shift in my understanding allowed me to become the kind of father I was proud to face in the mirror.

I wasn't one to adapt to fatherhood easily or quickly. I was largely absent, minimally involved with my children in their first two or three years. I couldn't believe parenting was supposed to be this hard or that I couldn't somehow master this change in my life.

Having accepted myself as a student around my children, I've found great joy in letting go of the notion that they are inferior. The privilege of supporting each individual in their own journey is an opportunity to be part of it all. This makes me grateful, and perhaps I can share a few insights along the way. Though our children come from us, we don't have the right to dictate how they express their essence. I do believe in providing them with principles, but I've become more detached from how they interpret those principles. Getting out of their way allowed me to give them a chance to experience life on their own terms. My reinvention has been integral to bridging the gap, so I can provide a runway to reaching their inherent highest and truest potential.

83

As a younger man, I felt masculine when impressing my friends, having sex with strange women and being ripped. Masculinity now means relevance, good citizenship, and being a loving father.

—Scott Galloway,
The Algebra of Happiness

This quote from *The Algebra of Happiness* has been extremely comforting to me, because I appreciate holding onto what was once satisfying. We go through different stages in life, and as I've matured, I've often found myself at crossroads where I longed for what was and feared that what is couldn't possibly offer the same fulfillment.

Writer Kurt Vonnegut once said, a step backward after making a wrong turn is a step in the right direction. This is how I view personal evolution. I've tried to relive past joys by seeking that same fulfillment. Sadly, it can never be the same. You pay for your new life with your old one. This has never been an easy transition for me. It's inevitable that we'll cross hundreds, perhaps thousands, of bridges on our journey to become the next version of ourselves. The evolution of your needs and fulfillment is one of the best things about growing up. Things that once held zero value bring me immense joy today.

Staying in on a Saturday night, watching my kids eat cereal and enjoy morning cartoons, receiving a hug from my wife, even growing my vegetable garden—these offer a smaller, yet more lasting fulfillment than I'd found in previous years.

In my case, I was an old infant. I believe I suffered from a form of the Peter Pan syndrome. I simply seemed unable to mature into adulthood. I behaved in a way that was devoid of responsibility and challenge. Yet there's no value in remaining a child, turning away from becoming more. Scott Galloway demonstrates that what fulfills us as children is inwardly focused, in contrast to the outwardly focused fulfillment you experience as an adult. The reality is, we'll spend the vast majority of our lives as adults. Unless, that is, we're the children who don't grow up.

When I started to find joy in relevance, good citizenship, and being a loving father, my life didn't just change. It began. Losing your youth doesn't mean you're losing the part of you that enjoys fun, spontaneity, or living in the moment. It just means you've discovered your usefulness supersedes your selfish ambitions. My unrealized potential had to be exchanged for the actual experience of becoming something. Once, I considered that to be a sacrifice. I've learned it's a small price to pay. It's only through my evolution into adulthood, and my new emphasis on outward focus, that I became capable of sustaining the joy and magic of youth for a lifetime.

84

You will be stronger because you fell and got up.
Be patient during the journey, if you rush your
healing you will not get the lesson.

—Olympia LePoint,
rocket scientist

Patience has never been my strong suit. I would rather make a thousand hasty decisions than take the time to make a single well-considered one. Despite my ability to take action quickly, I learned from Olympia Le Point that each time I fall and get up, there is a lesson easily overlooked. Christian preacher T. D. Jakes tells us that with every lesson comes a blessing. Others have pointed out that until one learns the lesson the first time, life will find a way to keep giving you grief, until one day you do decide to learn it.

When you experience pain or challenge, it can be difficult to remain patient and endure it. I dislike being uncomfortable. It's one of the reasons why this lesson continues to be presented to me on a regular basis. We must become comfortable with being uncomfortable. This is something I continue to work through, on a daily basis.

The key to discovering the reason for your fall is patience, which can be found only by accepting the lengthy healing process that follows a fall. Through introspection, you come to understand the decisions that led to your fall. This is hard, sometimes painful, work.

Looking back, you'll see things about your thought process and easily identify what you should have done.

Sometimes it's not pretty. If you're like me, you'll see how often you act on impulse or emotion rather than logic.

Don't hide from the results that led to your downfall. Begin the healing process by having the courage and patience to examine how you arrived at your current situation. Ask yourself what ridiculous things you've been saying or doing regularly that lead to the results you're presently getting. What's on the other side may not be pleasant to contemplate. Still, you must do some introspection. Sit with what you find, in order to properly point yourself in the right direction.

Olympia LePoint once said she didn't understand basic math. She thought she simply wasn't as gifted as the other kids around her. Today she's a rocket scientist. Her humility led her to simply ask her teachers and professors for help understanding basic terms and definitions. It was in doing this that she realized she was smart and, more importantly, capable. If you're not patient with your journey, if you rush your healing and quickly move onto the next thing, it robs you of what you can learn about yourself. That lesson may be the very thing that will prevent you from falling the next time.

85

Knowledge is power: You hear it all the time but knowledge is not power. It's only potential power. It only becomes power when we apply it and use it.

—Jim Kwik,
podcaster, writer, entrepreneur

My reading habits changed dramatically over the past eighteen months. I went from reading less than five books in a decade to reading more than 100 in a year and a half. When I first came across the quote, it reminded me how stagnant my mindset had become.

It seemed to me that books couldn't possibly offer anything that my daily life couldn't. Actually, this was me projecting my disdain for formal education and the notion that job training and street smarts were much better pathways to success. What could a book teach me that I couldn't extract from my own life experiences?

Life experiences can take you only so far. When I'd reached the peak of my career and found myself at that unavoidable glass ceiling, I started to ask myself why the things that had brought me to that place were no longer working. Someone who reads a book and doesn't apply it has no advantage over someone who's illiterate. This also assumes that someone like me might actually want to read a book, whereas I was unable to get to even that point. Reaching a peak in my life helped me envision a future that I didn't like.

I didn't know what was scarier, seeing exactly what my life would look like ten years into the future or seeing ten years into the future and having no idea at all what it would look like. The latter was obviously the better choice, but I had to pivot from the path I was on, the very path that had brought me success. I couldn't envision a world where I'd have to learn to understand what was outside my current sphere of influence.

Initially, I chose *Kitchen Confidential,* by Anthony Bourdain. I thought it would at least be a topic I could relate to, but what fascinated me was that I didn't take away anything about the culinary industry from it. Instead, I came away with a better understanding that all human beings are flawed. There is rarely a straight path to success. For the first time, I was able to see that books are intimate conversations with someone who has a message to offer. I felt I'd be able to get satisfaction from that interaction. After I realized I could read a book and walk away with useful knowledge, I was more proactive in my approach to life. I faced the world with a different type of gusto. As Jim Kwik said, it becomes power only when we apply it and use it.

The moment I started putting those lessons to use, things changed. I'd spent the greater part of my first thirty years of life being useful to just one person: me. I gained knowledge through experience but kept it secret.

Initially, I thought I'd gain new information to use for the benefit of my career, primarily. I discovered I could also gather new information for others and make it available to them free of charge. I rarely meet a person who doesn't want to learn something useful, but I've met many like myself who can't be bothered with making the effort. As Jim Kwik said, if knowledge is power, then learning is a superpower. Learning provides the foundation for both personal and professional development. Make use of your inherent potential by acquiring and applying knowledge. Insight is not only deeply satisfying, it has utility to those around you.

86

The greatest mistake we make is living in constant fear that we will make one.

—John Maxwell,
writer, speaker, pastor

I've enjoyed being a leader in my career, but I've always felt extremely self-conscious when I've been given opportunity. Most of my career has been spent managing teams or individuals with a great deal more experience than I had myself. My regular bouts of imposter syndrome led me to doubt if I was qualified to lead. Had I somehow managed to convince those in charge to put me in charge? Whenever I interacted with older employees, I made every effort to sound experienced and familiar with their roles and responsibilities, in order to advise them on how to accomplish certain tasks.

I was living a fallacy; that leadership was about being right. Knowing the answer, all the time. In addition to being ineffective, it did nothing to actually improve the lives or circumstances of my team members.

That illusion was short-lived, because it's only a matter of time before this mentality ensures that, on the day when the team does not perform or achieve certain goals, you will be held accountable. You will frantically look for others to blame.

Empathy is the key to great leadership. It's not necessary to flex your power when you are in charge. What you decide to do in that position of authority is what matters. The ego must be released, because people are not interested in how much you know until they realize that you care.

Empowering others to be their best selves, affording them every opportunity to develop and shine, these are rare privileges. John Maxwell once said that a good leader is a person who takes a little more than his share of the blame and a little less than his share of the credit. Once you can understand what drives others, you can help them align their personal goals and aspirations to the greater initiatives of an organization. Then you'll simply need to get out of the way for results to flow in.

I had been placed in charge, not due to how much I knew or how well I managed people, but rather because of my ability to connect with others and bring out their best. After realizing this, I began to find true fulfillment and success in my career. It was only feeding my self-importance to live in constant fear that I'd make a mistake. This fueled my belief that I was better than the people I was responsible for. I used to manage my employees by ensuring they did't ruin my chances of success. Ironically, this ensured little to no chance of success. Those you lead not only support you, they don't care if you make mistakes along the way, regardless of your age or experience, if you operate from authenticity and prioritize ensuring the success of others.

87

*Brothers don't let each other
wander in the dark alone.*

—Jolene Perry,
novelist

During my childhood, I often felt like my brother woke up with the intention of making my life miserable. I was constantly abused and bullied, physically and mentally.

In a conducted study, the family dynamics of 6,838 British siblings were tracked until the age of twelve. The findings revealed a tendency for firstborn children and older brothers to engage in teasing behavior toward their siblings, with jealousy over sharing identified as a potential contributing factor.

Oddly enough, this mirrors my perspective on my brother during my upbringing. Regardless of the times I endured physical teasing, I consistently interpreted it with positive intent. It was clear to me that he cared for me deeply.He was my brother, but he needed to find the right outlet to express that love. In the same way that I was going through my own journey as a kid, so was he. There was no question in my mind he just wanted to spend time with me and that his form of affection was, let's say, physical. There were moments when I would be getting pummeled but I'd hold a slight smile knowing my life wasn't in danger.

As someone bullied extensively growing up, I know the difference between real danger and a person holding back. My brother always held back. Although I don't condone physical violence or bullying, I believe you should always give family the benefit of the doubt. When I fell down at my best friend's house and needed more than seventy-five stitches, my brother came racing from our house on his bike, like a superhero. He came right up to me, crying and holding my sliced-open knee, doing everything he could to make me feel better, saying I love you, over and over.

I'll never forget that day. That one day, that one singular moment, made all the previous teasing into a reinforcement of my faith in my brother. This was what my brother truly thought of me. I was important to him. It doesn't matter what he says or does, I will always know this is the way he feels about me. When I need him, he'll stop what he's doing and rush to my side.

As Martin Luther King Jr. says, the beauty of authentic brotherhood is more valuable than diamonds, silver, or gold. Being a younger brother taught me the importance of perspective. I could have chosen to see all the bad that happened, that made up my story and reinforced my victimhood, but after that I became more and more attached to my brother. He not only came to my aid countless times throughout my life, he's also served as my mentor and guide. I've always looked up to my big brother and still do, particularly because just as I held positive intent for his actions as a child, he did the same for me through my darkest and not-so-kind years that I've imparted on him.

Don't write people off, especially family. It always takes two. There's a dynamic, and you're part of it even if you don't see it. Someone will always be giving, and someone will always be receiving. Be okay with whatever side you're on in the moment. This is key to nourishing the relationship.

88

Never before in our country's history has a generation been so empowered, so wealthy, so privileged—and yet so empty.

—Ben Shapiro, American writer, conservative political commentator

Those who have heard Ben Shapiro speak know how polished, quick-witted, and intelligent he is. I respect his point of view, because he's opened my mind with solid logic and relevant facts. He debunked many fixed beliefs I'd held about things, from politics to relationships. In his quote above, he was referring to the Millennial and Gen Z generations. These generations are heavily influenced by social media.

My own relationship with social media has not been great. I often looked at the posts of others and felt envy. I'd see my friends, family, or coworkers doing amazing things and think to myself, my life is subpar in comparison. "Comparison" being the key word here. I felt compelled to congratulate them anyway, which only compounded my feelings of inferiority.

This changed in 2019 when I decided to stop being active on social media. I'm not going to bash social media. There are tons of great things about it. It's a platform to help foster connection, learn new things, and share thoughts and ideas. In my experience, seeing someone's life on Instagram was what I thought life was like on a daily basis for them. Of course, I know it's merely a highlight reel. But it is up to the person consuming the content to keep in mind that a post is just one particular moment in their life, and I wasn't doing that.

A 2018 British study tied the use of social media to decreased, disrupted, and delayed sleep, which in turn is associated with depression, memory loss, and poor academic performance. I know lots of people who have a healthy relationship with social media, but I myself when engaging on the platforms became one of the statistics.

But what I've come to learn is I didn't necessarily have an unhealthy relationship with social media. I had an unhealthy relationship with my own self esteem. My behavior and traits were amplified by social media. In attempting to nourish my self-esteem, I found prioritizing self-care was the cure. I had to release myself from an unhealthy mindset, full of vanity and comparison. Instead of spending three to four hours a day on social media, I redirected that time to self-care activities that benefited both my physical and mental well-being. This included reading, meditating, exercise, or simply spending time with my loved ones. As Shapiro points out, when we use social media, we're subjected to extreme highs followed by extreme lows. The intense dopamine rush you receive from social media is the same as from a drug. The more you consume, the greater the craving.

My mindset has changed from one of lacking to one of abundance. This change happened as a result of prioritizing my own self-care. My feelings of emptiness began to disappear when I started my daily practice of gratitude daily for what I do have in my life. Comparing my life with someone else's caused me to believe I'd never be enough. However, you can never attain the level another person reaches. You can only attain the highest version of your own life.

That sense of emptiness was directly related to a lack of self-care.This led me to seek fulfillment in unhealthy ways. After spending so much time on social media, I came to realize it is my own life that I should watch so closely and admire.

89

Humility is not thinking less of yourself, it's thinking about yourself less.

—C. S. Lewis,
British writer

The first time I made $25,000 on a four-week project for my consultancy, my mind was blown. Having just advised a board of entrepreneurs and venture capitalists on where their company should focus to generate new revenue, I had reached the pinnacle of my career. At the time, however, I was unaware of how much my happiness was driven by external validation.

There's something sinister about receiving too much praise and too immediate rewards. Like a drug, they overrun you with euphoria, then quickly leave your body with withdrawal symptoms. That's how the week following my big consultancy project felt to me. The next month, I made the same amount of money and thought to myself, this isn't enough. No praises were given to me, nor were there any grand shout outs, and I felt pretty depressed. Only after speaking with a friend did I realize just how fortunate I was to have been given these opportunities.

The experience of hearing about another's struggles to break into their own business success was not only humbling, it was also humiliating. Deep down, I realized how much I valued my own self-importance. Making good money was no longer sufficient; now I also needed to be given a grand celebration.

In my sheer embarrassment, I started to talk to my struggling friend about his business. I spent the next month talking through with him various marketing and business strategies. For hours on end, I provided immediate value at zero charge, and it felt great. It reminded me of the reason I started the consultancy in the first place, to provide value to others in any way I could.

It has become evident to me that I have the ability to give back to others. With my consultancy's success, I can provide useful business insights and wield a new type of social influence. For the first time, people started telling me they wanted to create that same success for themselves.

Our actions and words have a profound impact on others' choices, especially if we embody a characteristic they wish to emulate. By removing my ego from my successes, I've not only remained grounded, but it has helped me focus on the utility I hope to provide to others. The advice my parents once gave me was, don't become conceited because of your success. If you were to change, we would be there to remind you of where you came from. I needed less praise and more advice like that.

You can get so caught up chasing success that one day, when you do achieve it, you want simply to bask in it. If you act with humility and grace after you have achieved success, it will define your character and offer you a fulfillment that lasts a lifetime. To avoid becoming a victim of your own self-importance, recognize that success is merely the outlet by which you offer value to those around you. With success, thinking less about yourself allows you to return to a state of being that is outwardly focused, which ironically is usually the doorway to success.

90

*If you aren't in over your head,
how do you know how tall you are?*

—T. S. Elliot,
poet

As kids, we go through stages. We don't usually think of them as challenges to overcome; we simply step forward. Going from elementary to high school to college to a full-time career, there is simply no way around the fact that things will be upside down and uncomfortable. In each new situation you enter, you recognize you are a beginner. You have no idea what lies ahead, possibly fighting an uphill battle with only a partial understanding of what lies ahead. But you move anyway.

When you're a child, someone feeds you, provides you with clothing, and someone pays your tuition. You grow up totally dependent on them. However, the acceptance is where the magic happens.

Accepting the journey, letting go of preconceived notions about how to get where you're going, is something beautiful. It's usually not in the moment when you're satisfied with your struggle, but rather in retrospect, after you've seen it through, that you feel a sense of fulfillment.

This happens over and over again for children. It becomes a part of their routine. Children are constantly learning new skills and facing new situations. They accept that they're in over their heads with everything they attempt. In adulthood, you choose to continue going

179

through those difficult scenarios. Or not. But putting clothes on your back, paying your tuition, keeping a roof over your head, and eating are all up to you.

T. S. Elliot believed that one doesn't grow old, but rather stands still and stagnates at a certain age. To maintain the momentum of childhood, it's essential to willingly immerse yourself in challenging situations, actively pushing your abilities to their limit in them. Actively creating my own struggle has been key to mastering my personal evolution, to surviving new challenges in life but also thriving in the face of uncertainty.

Learning a new language involves a total immersion experience, with no way out, and the necessity of doing away with the old. The only way to succeed is by activating something in your brain that was previously dormant. Your brain becomes ready not only to adapt but to thrive in the new environment. It never occurred to me that it would be possible to consume more than 1,000 hours of content in a year or that I could read an entire book in a few days, but in a total, almost overwhelming, immersion you lose all desire for ease and certainty. You open yourself to growth instead of seeing it as something to avoid.

91

Compelling careers often have complex origins that reject the simple idea that all you have to do is follow your passion.

—Cal Newport,
writer, professor

Though I was passionate about cooking, I didn't want to put in the hours it took to develop the skills necessary to truly excel in the culinary arts. I liked to make pastries. I enjoyed the art of artisanal bread making. I liked to cook meats on an industrial grill and the art of properly layering flavors in a slow stew. When my enjoyment collided with the obsession of another young chef, it became clear that my passion for becoming a chef wasn't enough to achieve the highest level of leadership and innovation.

This was defeating and demoralizing. People always tell you to follow your passion, but what they don't tell you is what you're passionate about may not be your greatest talent. Once, I held out hope that my passion would catapult me past my colleagues, who had devoted countless hours to their craft. If passion was supposed to drive my career, but it wasn't paying off, then what?

Having put no effort into exploring other career options, I was lost and confused. I found the next most obvious place to go for those who can't make it in a kitchen, the front of the house. Here, surprisingly, I discovered that I possessed raw talent, but not necessarily passion. I was great at speaking to guests, financially savvy, and had a natural aptitude for the meticulous planning required to manage a restaurant operation. I was not following my passion, but I was doing things for which I had a natural aptitude. This led me to a new career path.

According to Cal Newport, if you want to love what you do, abandon the passion mindset and adopt a craftsman mindset. A craftsman mindset is concerned with what you can offer to the world. I discovered I could offer the world my natural talents. By doing that, I was able to develop a passion. In order to develop my skills in the front of the house, I had to work hard, but I am convinced that if you are solely focused on what you are passionate about, you lose sight of your talents, talents that can one day blossom into passion and perhaps even a career.

They say that human beings are at their best when immersed deeply in something challenging. Doing something you don't naturally enjoy is where you break the mentality of doing only what you love when it doesn't present hardships. Don't let your passion get in the way of what your career could be. Align your natural talents with as many opportunities as possible, and when you discover one that hints at opportunity, accept the challenge and put forth the effort. It will reveal not only your passion, but also your path to success.

92

Learning, at its core, is a broadening of horizons, of seeing things that were previously invisible and of recognizing capabilities within yourself that you didn't know existed.

—Scott Young,
Ultralearning

Most of my life, I thought my learning abilities were fixed. Growing up as the class clown, there wasn't much discussion of me being anything other than entertaining or creative. At thirty-five, I began to tap into a new type of learning, what Scott Young calls ultralearning. Ultralearning is a strategy for aggressive, self-directed learning. The advantage of self-directed learning is that you take back control of your education rather paying expensive tuition. Aggressive means that instead of spending years at something without mastering it, your limited time and effort are always directed toward what works.

Young says the best ultralearners are those who blend practical reasons for learning a skill with the inspiration that comes from something that excites them. When I left my very safe job in corporate America to join a startup, this was exactly what I didn't know how to do. To survive, I was going to have to discover a different side of myself, someone who would be more than just a creative individual, but who could also offer skills such as analytics and strategy. It was a mixture of innate gut feeling that I was capable of more and a genuine curiosity as to whether I could actually evolve into someone new.

It was an experience that was both exciting and gut wrenching. To expand my ability to grow and develop new skills, I had to fully immerse myself in the unknown and the uncomfortable.

Most of us operate at about half of our capacity. Because we haven't experienced anything different, we assume that's what we're capable of. You don't achieve the deepest moments of happiness by doing easy things, you achieve them by realizing your potential and overcoming your self-limiting beliefs.

The new skills I developed through deep immersion and active practice are not necessarily things I hadn't ever done before, but they were things I told myself were not for me. For years, I believed that being analytical, strategic, or data-driven was for someone else. When I realized that not only could I develop these traits, but by doing so I would be able to develop even more skills I hadn't been confident enough to claim, such as leadership, financial acumen, and public speaking skills.

Ultralearning can become a positive obsession in your life if you're open to the journey. When you begin the process of discovering new skills and overcoming previously held beliefs about your limitations, the sheer fulfillment is so addictive you'll find yourself running out of avenues to apply them. Ultralearning ultimately led me to compete and place in a national weightlifting competition, become a vice president, establish a six-figure consulting firm, and spend more time with my wife and children. Using ultralearning caused me to wake up every morning at 3 A.M. I never view this as lost sleep, but rather as a way to make sure that my desire to learn new skills, and to break down limiting beliefs, is given as much time as possible to develop.

93

Rest until you feel like playing,
then play until you feel like resting, period.

—Martha Beck,
writer, life coach

It has always been my habit to overwork. When it comes to pushing my limits, I often don't realize when I've gone too far. Then my mind or body give out. I have an odd sense of mortality; I often feel that today is my last day on earth. This helped me foster an insane work ethic, with urgency and high standards for everything I do.

The flip side is that I tend to put the least amount of effort into resting. It was always my view that rest was simply that extra time between work hours. If that extra time actually results in rest, fine, but if not, I wasn't concerned. Even when you're not doing anything, you aren't necessarily getting rest. I realized this one year. I was traveling with my family and applying zero effort to rest or fun activities. That vacation was an eye opener. In all the other areas of my life, I would apply maximum effort to have the best quality output, but when it came to rest and relaxation I made a subpar effort.

I realize that it sounds a little crazy to put effort into rest, but on my final two days of a ten-day vacation, I did just that. I applied effort to figuring out how I wanted to relax and play. The work ethic I developed and applied toward fun activities wasn't able to make up for the other eight days of lost potential rest and enjoyment, but it more than compensated for that loss. Rest was something that just happens. I wondered why I never enjoyed it, felt guilty about it, and never returned from vacation feeling rejuvenated. When I began to see my rest as an investment back into myself, it became as valuable to me as my work.

By prioritizing and actually planning out my rest and fun, I live up to the idea of working smarter, not harder. When I don't rest and recover properly, my results stagnate. For years, I believed I needed to exercise seven days a week and eat 100 percent cleanly every day to achieve the physical results I desired. But muscles grow when you're not working on them, and our bodies naturally crave a balance of healthy and unhealthy foods. It's also important to make sure the type of rest you take is something you actually look forward to. Find the type of recovery that rests not only your physical body and mind, but importantly, nourishes your soul.

I am able to go for several months without needing to take time off, because the relaxation I do take is such a powerful form of rejuvenation. Be equally driven and apply the same level of energy and thought to rest and play. Ultimately, maximizing your rest maximizes your productivity.

94

Friendships are not light switches that you flick on and off when it's convenient for you or when you need it to serve you.

—Dandapani,
Hindu priest,
entrepreneur, former monk

I, for one, have a history of prioritizing my own needs well over anyone else's. I'm much better at minimizing this characteristic these days, but for years I've stomped, trampled, and manipulated friendships to meet my own selfish ends. I used to value having as many friends as possible, much like collecting art. One-sided value: merely something for me to admire and receive selfish satisfaction from. I would actively find ways to actually be as minimally involved with my friends as possible, asking myself, what's the bare minimum I need to do to sustain this friendship?

I was knee deep in my own personal hell of selfish behavior when my best friend asked me, what had happened to me? At one point, my friend continued, "I used to look up to you." It's definitely rock bottom when someone who truly sees you gives you a mirror. You see how you're showing up, and it is beyond gut wrenching.

You know your true friends when they walk into the room while everyone else leaves. I saw my friend's candor as the universe's way of affording me an opportunity to pay back some debts. I was given damn fine friends, who wouldn't let me live the crappiest version of myself, nor let me get off scot-free.

There were two options available to me. I could either continue down this course and simply rinse and repeat the cycle with all of my new friends. Or I could begin a journey of redemption, by showing up as my best self to those who were previously familiar only with my worst self. I put in the time and energy not only to repair these damaged friendships, but to accept a heavy dose of humility. For the first time, I had an opportunity to learn how to be on the giving end of a friendship. Even texting people back had been a big deal for me, but oddly enough, just doing it made me feel like a better person.

I'll spend the rest of my life on my quest to right the wrongs I did and the selfish acts I inflicted on so many of my closest friends. By doing so, I find I can afford the greatest gift I could want, which is perspective. Value those who believe in you. Those who always hold you to your highest version of yourself are treasures. They're the ones who will stop you from destroying yourself and sabotaging your life. Stick with the people who pull the magic, not the madness, out of you.

Dandapani recommends treating your energy the same way that you treat money; it's a finite resource that needs to be managed and invested wisely.

Today I'm not only mindful who I spend my time with, but I focus my full awareness on being with that person, aiming to be fully present and seeking to give. For all I've taken, I see nobility and, more importantly, purpose in giving it all back.

95

Strive not to be a success,
but rather to be of value.

—Albert Einstein,
theoretical physicist

Whenever I'm focused solely on success, or
making money, it never comes. If by some
chance it does come to fruition, it's rarely fulfilling. When
I established my consulting company, I had a simple
objective. I wanted to help my mentors, the key word
being "help." I considered my venture an opportunity to
help businesses and individuals reach their full potential,
and yes, it would also bring in good money.

In my consulting business, I can easily work between
25 and 30 hours over my regular work week of 60 to
70 hours. It wasn't an attempt to destroy myself or burn
myself out. Rather, I just kept pushing myself to maintain
the feeling of deep joy that comes from providing value
to others.

The more I was of value to individuals, the more value
I created for the company as a whole. I was astonished
at my work capacity. Whenever you act from a place
of giving, aiming only to be of value, you're rewarded.
You're granted the opportunity to draw from an unlimited
well of energy, creativity, and vision.

This has been referred to as the zone; the zone being
a state of full immersion and full engagement in what
you're doing. Further, it entails working at your peak

capacity while feeling fully fulfilled. To me, this process had seemed to be a once-in-a-while experience, like a runner achieving a runner's high, or something mysterious that just happens from time to time. Something elusive. But if you create value for yourself alone, your perception of time and energy becomes tainted, forcing you to operate in scarcity mode, limiting the possibility of entering the peak state. This in turn diminishes the opportunity.

Being able to enter this peak state is a powerful tool that can be applied to anything in your life at any given time and wielded at your discretion. For more than three years, I have woken up between 3 and 4 A.M. every morning. Operating from this peak state every day led me to quadrupling my income, starting a six-figure consultancy, generating a net worth of more than one million dollars, competing in Olympic weightlifting, completing an MBA with distinction, buying my dream car and new house, as well as being the best husband, father, brother, son, and friend I have ever known.

When I was solely focused on achieving my goals, wishing to attain wealth, things were always difficult and never achieved. Having a value-oriented mindset and striving to make a positive contribution to others allows you to reach your highest potential every day and hour, as well as gain incredible treasures along the way. When your sole input is driven by being of value, it will lead to sustainable success and unbelievable treasures along the way.

96

When you lose, talk little.
When you win, talk less.

—Tom Brady,
pro football player

Tom Brady, arguably the greatest quarterback of all time, has more right to brag about his accomplishments than most. He was undervalued at the beginning of his career, then criticized for achieving greatness late. He remained humble, and his quote resonated with me quite a bit.

No matter how large or small my accomplishments were, I have always sought to make them public as much as possible. I considered loudmouthing and displaying arrogance to be signs of confidence, even virtues. For years, family and friends have discreetly told me I'm arrogant and boastful, but in my mind, my accomplishments were inspiring others.

I felt that I was a beacon of light shining on something they too could achieve in their lives. But in fact, it was the exact opposite. It was not only humbling, but a reminder that my accomplishments are merely that, and self-importance is a fleeting feeling of achievement.

As I've gotten older, I've seen the beauty of winning with a purpose. An accomplishment that helps improve an individual's life, a community or even a business holds lasting value.

Pursuing praise was the very reason that satisfaction was temporary and unsatisfactory. At worst, praise is a delusional group acceptance with empty accolades. I still have moments when I would like to post my accomplishments on social media to attract likes, shares, and comments. However, any benefit it does bring is solely mine.

Theologian C. S. Lewis says humility doesn't mean thinking less of yourself, it means thinking of yourself less. Winning today means your unique gifts and individual contributions make a difference toward a goal that's greater than you are. When there's benefit that extends beyond yourself, there's not only nobility in that, but it's a way to stare at the very challenges in front of you and keep putting forth your best efforts. In being pulled toward a purpose, you receive praise for what you achieve along the way, but your accomplishments will never be as satisfying as when you're using your gifts and talents for something greater than yourself.

I used to have to prompt people with tales of what I've achieved in order to receive their praises. By operating from a place of humility and consistency, I no longer need to explain why I'm great. Greatness can be implicit, and it's through that silence that your achievements will be heard.

97

*The universe is under no obligation
to make sense to you.*

—Neil DeGrasse Tyson,
American astrophysicist

It's very human to attempt to make complete sense of our lives. It's easy to think we're in control of everything, when in reality there's possibility in every moment. Anything you would perceive as good—or bad —could happen. "Perceive" is the key word here. I've spent days, weeks, months, even years in a depressed state, thinking things are supposed to be different. Somehow my life wasn't what it should be. I wasn't where I could be.

The need for a perception of things, that they must be going a certain way, was what kept me always feeling inadequate. I would compare every aspect of my life to the progress and characteristics of others in a ridiculous and, frankly, incomparable manner. I'd ask myself why so many bad things happened to me and why so many good things happened for others.

The saying goes you're either entering a storm, in the middle of a storm, or leaving a storm. There is no doubt that life is full of challenges and struggles and that we have nearsighted perceptions, often clouded by emotions. It's nearly impossible to grasp how valuable are the lessons you've learned in your seasons of change.

Astrophysicist Neil DeGrasse Tyson says that if you want to assert a truth, first make sure it's not just an opinion that you desperately want to be true. I've had many moments when I was trying to fit a square peg into a round hole, by attempting to fit all my unique life experiences, aspirations, and goals into a framework that wasn't built for me. I tended to pay close attention to every twist, turn, and bump along the way. I had no clear vision of where I was heading.

Today I stay focused on my purpose, my *why*, or what I know deep down I'm called to do in this life. This helps me pay less attention to the sheer chaos that ensues in our day-to-day lives. A heat-seeking missile maintains its trajectory only by constantly changing its course. Mini-servo mechanisms adjust the missile based on negative feedback. It will continually making these adjustments until it reaches its target.

In order to move forward, you must keep making adjustments to your life. The moment you realize that each of these challenges was exactly what kept you moving forward, you'll look back on your life and realize that each was precisely the obstacle necessary to keep you on track.

98

If you can dream it,
you can do it.

—Walt Disney,
animator, film producer,
entrepreneur

I used to stay up at night and imagine how my life would one day turn out. The older I got, the more uncomfortable I felt. Shouldn't that one day have already happened? It was easier to imagine what my life would look like when being an adult was years away. I'd look around me and see others doing things I knew I could do. Then I'd imagine what my adult life would look like if I did these things also.

My dreams became more difficult once I began to attempt to fulfill them. I used to think that when someone embarks on a quest to pursue their deepest desires, they would be aided by a magical force that would carry them through to the end.

Not only was I wrong, but I also developed resentment toward myself for having such high expectations. It began when I returned to school to earn my bachelor's degree while raising a newborn, a two-year-old daughter, holding a full-time job, competing in CrossFit, and being a fully dedicated husband. My first assignment nearly broke me. It was difficult, and there was no easy way out.

When we think about accomplishing our deepest desires we often don't imagine the road to get there. As obstacles presented themselves along the way, I became increasingly unsure of why I was trying to accomplish these things in the first place. But I had already paid my tuition for the current year, so there seemed no turning back. At school I was unable to walk away from my dream. Putting myself in a position where I couldn't walk away proved to be crucial to my success.

Walt Disney also said, the difference between winning and losing is most often not quitting. When I became fully invested in making my dream a reality, I began discovering new abilities in myself. Doing the hard things daily began to transform who I was. I realized that to achieve my wildest dreams, I couldn't do it as the current me.

Character is formed by what you do on your third and fourth tries. Failing repeatedly and facing hardship helped me develop a new mindset and, ultimately, a new self. When I did graduate, it was satisfying knowing I could accomplish what I set out to do. It sparked a cascade of new endeavors and challenges where I could test those new found abilities.

When I reflect on all the dreams that have come true since then, it's not the tangible results I admire, but knowing I can accomplish my wildest dreams.

99

Growing apart doesn't change the fact that for a long time we grew side by side; our roots will always be tangled. I'm glad for that.

—Ally Condie,
writer

I used to think once you forged a strong bond with someone, a great friendship had begun and it would always stay that way. When inevitably closeness faded, I often blamed the other for changing and ruining everything. Or somehow, perhaps, neither of us really cared about the other. Losing contact with someone I grew up with took me a long time to accept. I've realized that just because you and your friend are no longer side by side, it doesn't necessarily mean you've drifted apart. As Ally Condie points out, there will always be tangles in the roots.

I look back with such reverence on the times when I grew up with someone. Knowing our roots will always be tangled gives me an assurance that no matter how far I may be from someone so dear to me, in the course of our lives the tangled roots will change their structure forever. Without tangled roots, we wouldn't be as strong as we are. We wouldn't have the very important life lessons that were born from our interaction. Water, so to speak, continues to nourish us through the root system, which enables that very growth into a new network. The valuable lessons I bring from previous interactions are woven deeply into my life.

I've learned to appreciate being truly close to someone as a gift. It's important to stay connected to old friends, because they alone offer the perspective of the version of yourself that was key to who you are today.

Moments of connection with a person from my past provide me with a deeper understanding of who I used to be. They're the only conduits through which I'm able to access those early lessons, making them all the more meaningful. They serve as a reminder of my personal evolution. Remembering past perspectives reminds me what it's like to not be who I am today, simultaneously affirming today's direction.

The fact that you have grown apart from a friend means you've both become responsible for the growth of others and for the growth of larger communities. Every earlier version of me was good enough for that friend and still lives within their memory. This has been my redemption during the darkest days of my life. I know I've been of immense value to someone once, and therefore have much potential for bringing value to others in the future.

100

*Your biggest problem is
that you think you shouldn't have one.*

—Tony Robbins,
entrepreneur, life coach

Tony Robbins once told a story about flying his jet helicopter to a seminar. He found himself flying directly over a building where he'd worked as a janitor just ten years before. At the time, it was impossible for him to predict the outcome of pushing through his current struggles. Looking back, however, it was the only way for him to end up hovering over that very building nearly a decade later. It's so easy to assume that when you set out to do something, it will be a straight line.

The moment I hit my first setback toward achieving a goal, I often got discouraged. I interpreted that as a message from the universe telling me to turn around. Having actually achieved my goals over the years, the main difference I've observed is that, when that first setback occurs, it is the universe's way of telling you need to make a pivot to continue. It's telling you you have the option of turning back or accepting this challenge in order to move forward.

Robbins once said that some people hunker down and wait out the storm of winter, while others go skiing. As with everything else, challenges are inevitable, but they also present opportunities for growth, which is what makes achieving something for the first time so rewarding.

Aside from getting from point A to point B, you grow and change as a person, becoming more capable, more knowledgeable, and more adept at facing new challenges in life. When you decide to pursue something, really decide to pursue it, you have to accept all challenges along the way as a necessary part of the process. When you choose only the easiest parts of a journey, you cannot expect the same rewards and fulfillment at its end.

In many cases, we're more concerned with the cost of what we want than with the actual object of our desire, so when you begin to weigh the difficulties into your decision, your dream begins to fade.

Think of all the things in life that you've already accomplished. It's unlikely that any lasting value came easy. Challenges are a unique gift, given to you so you can give that story back to the world. If you're willing to change who you are along the way, the universe will offer you both challenges and rewards.

There are a number of things I'd never want to relive, but would also never change, because I've grown so much from them. It often takes years for that perspective to set in, so think about what challenges you're facing today and remind yourself there's a future with a better life, counting on you to accept today's adversity.

101

Be impeccable with your word.

—Don Miguel Ruiz,
The Four Agreements

The basic idea behind this part of *The Four Agreements* is that when we speak or even think a particular thought, we've made an agreement with ourselves, a perception and a way of being that directs our actions. What we say to ourselves matters. What we think matters. Our words are the momentum that pushes our lives forward. Depending on the conversation you're having with yourself—or the agreement—you'll operate to ensure that it's true.

My life has been characterized by a lot of self-criticisms. I've allowed people to abuse me, fearing that otherwise I wouldn't be accepted. I was in a negative system that rewarded my submissiveness with the approval of others, but at the expense of living in a way where I could have been treated better.

As far as I was concerned, I wasn't worth attention or affection unless I behaved a certain way. To gain acceptance, I would lose more and more of my identity. I had crafted an agreement where I was not good enough to be myself. I should conceal that person from the world, because in my mind, my true self was unworthy, ugly, and not someone people wanted to see. In attempting to shed who I was, I found more and more of who I was not. Through trying on various personas over the years, I discovered that humor was my outlet for being accepted by the majority. Through a new agreement, where I was a funny person, I actually became funny.

During grade school and high school, I manifested years of laughter. The agreement I made with myself was to always be funny, no matter what. This gained me a lot of popularity and many friends. It didn't matter if I was hurting inside, sad, or even angry, being funny gave me the reward of acceptance and adoration. In the same way that I bullied myself into fitting into what I thought I should be, I would do the same for others. By labeling them ugly, dumb, or sad, I would influence them to think a certain way. Today I deeply regret those words. I'm sure they became someone else's disempowering self-agreement.

I make sure, now, to think about my words well before I ever say them. Choosing self-empowering words that help you to express the truest version of yourself and using those very words to help build others up is often highly undervalued.

Don Miguel Ruiz reminds us to speak with integrity. Say only what you mean. Avoid using a word to speak against yourself or to gossip about others. Be mindful of how you're speaking to yourself and about others; you never know whose very vulnerable life is under the power of your word.

102

The limit is not the sky, it is the mind.

—Wim Hof,
Dutch motivational speaker

Wim Hof, renowned for his extraordinary feats such as climbing Mount Everest in shorts and enduring a ninety-minute ice bath, has set more than twenty-six world records. Aptly named the Iceman for his ability to undertake challenging tasks, particularly in extreme cold, he advocates the untapped potential of the human mind. Despite never enduring an ice bath longer than five minutes or summiting Everest, I've witnessed my body accomplish what once seemed impossible by mastering my mind and silencing self-doubt.

In moments where I silenced my mind and embraced activities far beyond my comfort zone, my most significant personal growth unfolded. Wim Hof's breathing techniques, designed to seize control of our physiology and instill mental calmness, empower us to confront any situation objectively, free from negative mental influence.

When aspiring to run a six-minute mile, a goal challenging for the average thirty-six-year-old running an eleven-minute mile, Wim Hof's breathing exercises enabled me to quiet my mind amid pain. This mental composure allowed me to push myself, adapting to the intensity and consistently achieving 6:05–6:10 mile times daily.

Although the brain has been around for thousands of years, despite our evolution in physical form, humans still have a mind that protects them and prevents them from suffering pain. In the past, this was fine when avoiding things like sabertooth tigers, but with those elements gone today, our minds are still looking for other ways to avoid that pain.

You may be convinced that, not only are you not capable of certain physical feats, but if you attempt them, you will suffer serious consequences. But your mind doesn't know any better. It's doing its job. When you listen to it you've already lost. However, because the mind can be so powerful, it can also propel you confidently toward a task when you instruct it to remain silent. Just because your mind tells you to stop doesn't mean that your body can't keep going.

Wim Hof says we are the alchemists of our own bodies, meaning we can turn nothing into something. For years I wasn't a fitness enthusiast and people never knew me for anything related to physical prowess. Today, through constantly putting my mind and it's limiting beliefs through a meat grinder, I've realized anything is possible, not just physical accomplishments. Wim Hof's breathing techniques have helped me to realize that my own fears are a natural process.

When you face the fear that you know is deep down inside and stop running from it, you begin the process of dealing with it productively. Respecting the very struggle you're in allows you to acknowledge you're about to grow and take on something new. The beauty of this is that simply acknowledging there's an obstacle in front of you, merely attempting to face it by getting your mind and body in tune, carries over to all other aspects of life. Being confident in one's ability to face inner doubt ultimately translates to being confident in one's ability to face the world.

103

If you want to take the road to independence and happiness, find the right person to depend on and travel down the road with that person.

—Amir Levine and Rachel S. F. Heller, writers

In their book about attachment, Levine and Heller figure out how we fit into a few categories, and why we behave the way we do, particularly when we are in a romantic relationship. Generally, three types of people are identified: those who are secure in their relationships, which comprises roughly half of the population, those who are anxious in their relationships, and those who are avoidant in their relationships, which constitutes the remaining half.

For years I was taught that dependency was the mark of a weak man. In retrospect, I simply engaged with the world as I believed strong men should. If you've ever heard of the term "f*ckboy," it refers to those who hold a singular trait that makes them desirable to most women, which is the fact that they don't want to settle down. The fact that they are avoidant makes them nearly irresistible to women. As such, when I found that I could meet women easily by being independent or rather, avoidant, it only reinforced that this was a good thing.

My wife was the first person I wanted to share my life with and open myself up to, but didn't know how. I cringed at the idea of being so close that she might see my true self. It was difficult to open up about my insecurities.

I wondered how she was so ready to begin building a life together, while I was always telling her that one day I'd be ready, just not today.

This came crashing down as we entered nearly eight years of marriage and had our first child. It was supposed to be the moment where I'd fully embrace being a family man and get closer to my spouse and newborn daughter. But for me, it was the exact opposite. I wanted to run. I wasn't just afraid I would lose my independence, I was sure it was already gone. Now that she and I were parents, we had a little one to bind us forever. I had become the caregiver that another human was deeply dependent on.

It took me nearly five years to realize that my avoidant tendencies were a poison in my life that prevented my relationships from flourishing. I lost some of the most precious years of my baby girl's infancy, because I was even afraid to get too close to her. When my friends started to have kids, I began asking myself what special gene they had that allowed them to love both their spouse and children the way they did. That's when it became apparent that in order to have the relationships I wanted, I had to change.

Today I see the strength in not being independent, knowing that dependency strengthens independence instead of inhibiting it. We must allow for bonds to flourish and develop the deep roots of connection and intimacy. Being avoidant for many years allowed me to be independent, but it also robbed me of the special joy and connection that came with relationships. I spent the vast majority of life staring vulnerability in the face while standing behind an image of having it all together.

There's a balance between independence and dependence. Acknowledging where you are between the two is the first step in truly allowing your relationships to reach their maximum potential. In this way you'll experience fully all the richness that deep connection offers. Accept that your need for independence prevents you from offering love and enjoying all the love from others.

104

*Results are not the attainment of greatness
but the confirmation of it.*

—Brian P. Moran and Michael Lennington
The 12 Week Year

I've always believed that when I achieve something, then I will be successful. One of the most valuable lessons I've learned is that greatness can only be achieved when you begin the journey and consistently make the choice to accomplish difficult tasks. Those difficult things may be small and seem insignificant in the moment, but accumulated over time they create your pathway to success. I liked this notion, because it reminded me that I can be great today. I don't have to wait until my goal is achieved, I can be proud right here right now.

I spent years living in the ups and downs between achievements. A great accomplishment would make me feel alive, and I would allow myself to be happy and fulfilled when I'd done something of such magnitude. The problem with this is, those moments are mostly far and few between. It's hard to admit, but for many of us, life is lived trying to jump from peak to peak and often avoided when you're in the valleys. I've spent years between attained goals, which were simply bland to me. In contrast to the time spent basking in my own glory after achievement, I'd get frustrated and impatient when I was supposed to be working toward something.

The hardest thing to do is to know how hard you have worked today and not see the results immediately, then wake up the next day and do it all again, in the belief that continued effort will eventually bear fruit. There's an honor and nobility in picking up your suffering daily. Working toward something that doesn't come easy helped reprogram my mind that being great doesn't always feel great in the moment.

The journey to greatness is often a lonely one, where only you are capable of recognizing its value. When you've achieved this goal and the results are evident, others will usually celebrate your greatness, but the greatness began long before you ever reached your goals. We've all heard it before, that a little bit makes all the difference or that grinding through pain will yield the best results, but truly embracing the hardship of the journey is something special worth developing.

It is gratifying and enjoyable to attain any goal when you've become less concerned with the results and have adopted the daily struggle for hard work, patience, and perseverance. Achieving your goals and having others celebrate with you becomes icing on the cake, as the real reward is you've developed the ability to thrive during times of difficulty, particularly when your challenges are self-imposed.

105

The only difference between the saint and the sinner is that every saint has a past and every sinner has a future.

—Oscar Wilde,
poet and playwright

When I came across this quote it made me well up one morning. There's an immense sense of guilt in me for having been selfish, manipulative, unkind, and arrogant for so many years toward the most important people in my life. When I read this quote, I gained hope and faith in the possibility of one day becoming something other than the sum of my past behavior. I used to believe these traits were inherent in me, a curse of selfishness ingrained in the core of who I am, something that I would never be able to escape. I've seen where being the worst version of yourself leads.

Yes, seeing your not-so-great actions does not feel good, but what is truly sickening is being completely fine with it. When the behavior has become second nature and a normal way of being is when the numbness sets in. The moment your baseline behavior falls below any normal standard, things become scary. Like an addict experiencing withdrawal, your only solution to the numbness is to increase the intensity of terrible actions and behaviors that now give you your identity. The fun in starting down a dark path is that, deep down, you know there's a way out; this is just one act going against your moral convictions. It's not representative of who you are.

Unfortunately, it is not so fun when those you care about don't associate your behavior with your individual actions, but instead come to fully accept this not-so-great version of yourself. It may sound disgusting, but being horrible to people was like getting high on a drug for me; the more people tried to steer me away from bad behavior, the more I went in the opposite direction. But when there is no longer anyone to chase you, it has become a self-fulfilling prophecy.

I had two choices of what my future was going to be, more of exactly what got me here or something new. The key to my ascent from rock bottom has been accepting 100 percent of my past behaviors. Your past is not who you are; it's who you were. I give meaning to the past experiences by living extremely mindfully today and being conscious of my behavior so I never repeat past regrets.

By participating in this intervention, I learned that being aware of one's daily actions is where one can cast their vote for who he or she wants to become and reshape one's inner dialogue. I came to a realization through this agency that each one of us is both a sinner and a saint at some point in our lives. It all depends on how we view those actions and what we decide to do with it.

106

Don't be afraid to take time to learn. It's good to work for other people. I worked for others for twenty years. They paid me to learn.

—Vera Wang,
fashion designer

As far back as I can remember, I've looked up to others who were in successful positions or who had accomplished things I admired. I wanted to be them. Throughout my career and personal life, I've often bitten off more than I could chew and been immediately humbled when I realized the challenges others had had to overcome.

My successes have come from distancing myself from what I want and accepting that if I were willing to hone my craft enough, my time would come. My tendency is to glamorize others' successes and compare their unique paths with my own. It's always a losing proposition. The moment I become courageous and humble enough to open up to how I got there, my selfish ambitions seemed to fade away, and interestingly enough, when I stopped trying to attain that success the door actually opened and gave me the runway to reach it.

There's an idea from Alan Watts called the "backwards law." He teaches that the more you pursue feeling better all the time, the less satisfied you become, because pursuing something only reinforces the fact that you lack it in the first place. After disconnecting from the end goal and becoming obsessed with honing my skills, I was able to open door after door that led to the establishment of my own consultancy. Like Vera Wang, getting paid to learn is a gift if you are able to reframe your perspective. If you're willing to absorb as much information as possible from as many people as possible, one day you'll be the one providing guidance for others.

There is no precise moment when that happens. I do know that something special happens when you begin caring more about the work than the outcome. Acting with intent and avoiding attachment to the final outcome is the needed reframe that allows you to get through the most challenging of tasks. It's okay to be a student, it's humbling, and yes, sometimes it stings, but constantly being a student is where you will always draw your best efforts. Having lived this way has allowed me to not only achieve the success I have always dreamed of, but also to be content with where I am in my journey toward that success. As people come to realize how much you care, they'll be more inclined to value your knowledge and will compensate you for it without your asking.

107

*The worst thing you can do for your loved ones
is to try to reduce their pain.*

—Michael Gervais,
psychologist

Due to her journey being so different from mine, I kept thinking that when we got married, I was supposed to be my wife's knight in shining armor, because she had been through so much. My natural tendency is to solve problems and attempt to correct problems I see in front of me. In many ways, this is my way of avoiding difficult tasks. Being there and not trying to solve a problem is the hard part. To simply be a shoulder to lean on or a sounding board where she can voice her concerns as needed is hard, because it's uncomfortable. The desire of my heart to fix her or to find a solution to her problems was not only contrary to what she wanted, it was also contrary to who she needed me to be.

Being there for someone isn't always about solving their problems. In many ways, it's just being there with them. It's like you're a silent partner they can lean on as they work through it themselves. I tend to marginalize these issues by offering useless quotes about overcoming obstacles that I've read in books or on the Internet. These words would always fall flat.

There's both a freedom and a fulfilling purpose that comes as you decide to take the journey with them. It may take weeks, months, or even years, but you must not try to fix it. You must aim to support. As I thought to myself, I kept wondering why she could not move on, why she couldn't just simply be like me. I would get frustrated that she was dealing with things in a different way than my own, but this type of thinking only further isolated her from me.

I found my very nature to constantly try to fix only further reinforced my lack of empathy, thereby tainting any advice I would offer as only aimed at quickly solving her problems so they would no longer impact me. I am not responsible for someone else's happiness, but I should hold myself accountable to be there for that someone. I should be willing to disrupt my own peace of mind on the chance that it's the payment required for someone else's peace of mind. It's a hard thing to do, to willingly sit through the muck with someone, but it's the right thing to do. What kind of life would any of us have if all we did was live for ourselves, selfishly being always content or happy with our own circumstances, ignoring the troubles of those most important to us?

Today I don't try to ever take away someone's pain. I'm actively willing to sit with them through it, however long that may take. There's enormous value and comfort in spending time with someone in the arena of life, despite the fact you may or may not ever be rewarded for it. That's okay, because in this way alone, you are bringing the very comfort you are hoping to provide.

108

Whatever you are, be a good one.

—Abraham Lincoln,
16th president of the United States

As soon as I got married, my identity shifted from a single man to a husband. Every action I took was aimed at being the very best husband I could be. The examples I used were taken from people I knew and from TV shows or movies I had seen. When my entire identity was wrapped around this notion, everything was either fulfilling that vision or falling short. Because of my own self-imposed expectations, I lived in constant anxiety. The quote above reminds me of how hard I tried to be just one thing and how this ultimately led to me losing myself entirely.

Years ago, I'd interpret this quote to mean that success is achieved by mastering something. However, when I became only this one thing, I inadvertently became less in other areas that were equally important to me. Trying to be the best husband was not a bad idea, but it was not the idea that would allow me to be my best self in all areas of my life. My focus on being a great husband was too narrow, because when things went well, I had a sense of direction, but when things did not go well, I became disoriented. It was through this disorientation that I realized I had tied my self-esteem to my wife's happiness. When she was unhappy, I was not only disoriented, but worthless as well. As a result, I would do everything I could to regain my sense of self, which in itself is simply grasping onto whatever can be found at hand rather than being driven by a sense of purpose.

Instead of simply being a good husband, I chose to be a great man, achieving a wholeness that encompasses every aspect of what makes a good man not just one thing. I found a more fulfilling life when my aim wasn't only to be of value to one person, but to first focus on how I could achieve the highest version of myself so I could bring as much value to as many people as possible. Through this change in mindset, I was able to become more useful to those in my life who didn't necessarily know me only as a husband. The daily effort of being guided by this compass led me inadvertently to actually become a better husband, father, brother, son, and friend.

It took me years to grasp the concept that those who care for you don't want you to be a version of yourself, but to simply be. When I got my own life together, I was much more able to offer myself to others and still be of value to my wife. That is still important. Regardless of what you are, certainly aspire to be good at it, but make sure what you are becoming provides nourishment to all aspects of your life. Being one thing should not be at the exclusion of everything else.

109

*Real knowledge is
to know the extent of one's ignorance.*

—Confucius,
Chinese philosopher

Having experienced relatively moderate career growth, followed by exponential career success, I am able to view myself objectively. Depending on the situation, I may be seen as a solution to an executive's problems. In another way, I may be one of those newbies who realize they are in the room, but they don't yet have a place at the table.

This can be a hard pill to swallow on those days where some people hang on every word you say while others question why you're even speaking. My own ego was the thing that gave me confidence in my younger years, telling me stories of how I'm actually better than I was. But that same ego brought me chaos when I applied it to situations later in life.

I recall being in a situation with a young CEO where we didn't agree on marketing strategies. I kept thinking to myself that she was wrong. I was right. I handle marketing for Fortune 500 companies, what did she know?

In retrospect, I simply didn't have the answer to her problem. I clung on for dear life to the same value I normally had with other executives. Thinking deeper, if I'd actually ended up working with her, not only would I have been unqualified for the job, I would likely have only

217

been fulfilling my own selfish aim for validation. The real knowledge I acquired in that situation was that I'd been seeking the validation that I was good enough to work in any industry. Whether or not I would actually provide value wasn't even on my mind. Besides not adding value, my desire to be right and take control may have impeded the progress of that group and derailed their momentum.

It is an art to know what you are good at. Knowing when it's my turn to gracefully bow out is something that cuts deeply into my own ego on a regular basis. Today as I meet more and more executives, I aim to be as humble as possible on entering the room. I never know what they know, nor if my skill set would be of value to them. Knowing my limitations has been hard to grasp, because most of the time I tend even to surprise myself with my ability to succeed. The ability to own both your brilliance and your ignorance enables you to be everything to a select few, but you will never be everything to everyone in every situation. I don't enjoy admitting when I'm ignorant, but the harm of concealing my ignorance could leave a path of destruction in my wake.

110

Your existence is evidence that this generation needs something that your life contains.

—Myles Munroe,
Bahamian evangelist

There are many quotes out there regarding life's purpose, but this is one that resonates the most with me. It offers a broad message that eases my anxiety about my contribution to this world. I'm the first to say that one should have a purpose in life, but I have a hard time defining exactly what that entails. What I have found to be useful, however, is simply doing the right thing by my own standards. It's easy to assume that we make choices every day that impact our lives and those close to us, but the truth is, the ripples of our decisions extend far beyond the epicenter of our actions. We never know the impact our actions have on the world when we make choices that shortchange our potential.

I cannot necessarily link world peace to my actions, but I do know that if I choose not to choose violence or hatred on this planet, I contribute to the momentum of countless others on this earth and that my choice may provoke others to do the same, and so on. My purpose today is still somewhat unclear, but I do know that there's a general alignment between wanting good for this world and doing things daily to help create that future. Even if it's to simply to avoid doing things that I know will add more damage to this world. Upholding my own highest version of myself, I like the idea that my time on earth is meaningful and that there's a hidden gem I may never encounter where my life holds meaning that supports something far greater than myself.

Myles Munroe said once that most people die at age twenty-five and are buried at age sixty-five. It's a fairly depressing notion, but I know that there are certainly years between now and when I was twenty-five that were a blur. I simply didn't attempt to see the beauty in life, even in my tiny part of it. I therefore had no real reason to attempt to help re-create that beauty for anyone else. Taking daily actions toward a vision that may not come to fruition may seem like a futile goal, but it is through those daily actions that we give meaning and context to our life's highs and lows. In an ideal setting, future generations will be able to credit my small or even difficult daily life choices to create a better world. The idea allows me to live a fulfilling existence, knowing that I may have contributed to the planting of a tree under whose shade I will never sit.

111

Putting things off is the biggest waste of life: it snatches away each day as it comes, and denies us the present by promising the future.

—Seneca,
Stoic philosopher

The promise of the future has always been more appealing to me than the present moment. In many ways I've seen the present as simply a means to an end, doing today what I must so that I can one day receive my future rewards. The notion of living every day as if it is your last is a timeless one, but living each day like it's my last seems reckless to me. I might consider base jumping from a bridge, quitting my job, or scaling Mount Everest if today were indeed my last. Those are extreme things I would probably not actually do.

I lived on the other end of that spectrum for many years, fingers crossed for future pleasures, knowing I would likely wake up tomorrow, in the hope of getting closer to my future state. It was only when I encountered a difficult period in my life a few years ago, where my future appeared uncertain, that I began to appreciate the present day more. Considering the fact that my behaviors and patterns were ultimately leading me to a future I didn't want, it gave me the perspective that maybe today I could live better than tomorrow.

This was a key idea in my life. If the future was great, today didn't matter, but if the future seemed bleak, then today was all that mattered. The Stoic philosophy helped me understand there is opportunity in adversity, to accept situations as they are and move forward rather than hoping for a better future.

This idea that today is all I have and tomorrow I will be gone is not a new notion in my life. What is new for me is that the future I long for could very well turn out to be a complete disaster, as much as it could very much turn out to be the dream I've hoped to realize.

All of this points to the fact that regardless of the outcome, today—whatever your circumstances are—is all you have. If you can accept those circumstances and embrace every bit of your present condition, you'll have the best chance not only to get closer to your future aims, but to actually get a taste of them.

I thought the future held the relationship of my dreams, the future was where I'd be wealthy, or the future was the place where I wouldn't feel anxiety, sadness, or depression. Future promises are dangerous fallacies to fall prey to. I've come to realize that the future moment is right in front of me, available to me at any moment.

If you want to be wealthy, do something today that helps you get there. Act today in a way that your future self would act if you wanted a healthier, more loving relationship. Living the actions of my future self not only provided me with a greater understanding of what matters, it led me to realize that the present is the only place where I can experience my dreams, albeit one day at a time.

112

*What if you surrender and you didn't get less,
you got more?*

—Kute Blackson,
speaker, transformational teacher

'Ve always viewed surrender as a loss. It's something
that a coward does, something one does when
they've no other option to save themselves. The last few
words of the above quote were the most helpful part
of my understanding of this concept. I just didn't know
about it for nearly thirty years. This is exactly what I found
when I began to reframe my relationship with surrender:
to save myself. As an alternative to losing out, Kute
Blackson suggests we consider what would happen if we
surrendered and instead had a great experience. By not
trying to conform life to the specific and often unrealistic
way we think it should be, we end up attracting new
experiences into our lives, and things that normally go
unnoticed become more apparent.

There is, however, a component that must be
discussed here, namely the grief phase. Most people don't
know this about surrender. When you begin the journey
to fully accept what could be, you inevitably come to the
point where you must say good-bye to your hopes and
dreams, or at least as you think they should come to pass.

Surrender is still a very hard phase for me. Letting
go of how it comes to pass is particularly scary, because
I tend to live my life sequentially, one major event linked

to another. If one event doesn't happen as planned, then my plan is inherently off course.

As with grieving the loss of a loved one, this stage is essential for growth. I've found it's okay to be sad, even depressed, that I've surrendered. It is important to let that emotion pass through you, because without it, you'll always hold onto what has been and never give room to what could be. Kute reminds us that if we don't move toward surrendering, then we can't move forward to what our life has waiting for us.

Surrendering must also be a fully honest process. You can't pretend to surrender and still hope deep down that it will happen. You must completely let go, because surrendering with conditions and attachment is not surrendering at all. It is in fact self-deception.

When I surrender to the process, I find it has not derailed my dreams. Instead, it becomes the path through which my life accelerates toward those dreams, though now on a road I didn't know existed. Today my relationship with surrender is not one of cowardice. I must remind myself that it is a disguised act of bravery.

113

Dating is about grand romantic gestures that mean little over the long term. Marriage is about small acts of kindness that bond you over a lifetime.

—Lori Gottlieb,
writer, psychotherapist

During our first year of dating, my wife and I spent our entire paychecks on gifts for each other. The gifts seemed appropriate at the time, but each year it became increasingly difficult to top the gift of the previous year. Every time I thought of what I could do to show her my true love, I constantly considered what could be bigger, grander, and more extravagant than the last time.

The problem with this is that the more you focus on a singular action that brings about a singular positive reaction you tend to overlook the dozens, maybe even hundreds, of times each day when you could bring about that same reaction, just on a smaller scale. The problem is not only in the overwhelming focus on a single event, but also in the fact that it diverts your attention from those daily meaningful interactions.

These gestures also helped me balance the scale, allowing me to put forth minimal effort on a daily basis, because I knew I could just compensate for them during those few times a year. Just as Lori Gottlieb says, they not only mean less over time but the mere act of maintaining this habit makes the gesture itself routine, regardless of its extravagant nature.

Almost a decade after we began dating, I started doing the small things. I put forth less effort toward the big ones. It might have been something as simple as making her a cup of coffee when I made one for myself, giving her a new towel when I changed mine, or even asking if I could make her a plate when I served myself. Seems simple enough right? Wrong. The experience was not only difficult, but also painful. I would often wonder what was wrong with me, why I couldn't simply do things that weren't beneficial to me. Nor could I stomach the fact that these small acts might not even be acknowledged.

My conclusion was that I was not only looking for validation from my acts of love, but I was simply lazy. I had my moment of clarity during one of the most trying times in our relationship, the birth of our second child. If you are a parent of two children, you're well aware of how much a first child directly affects your relationship, let alone considering a second. I began to realize that my grand gestures were meaningless. Not only did she not care about them, but I was too lazy even to perform them.

If the large gestures weren't on the table, and I was still inherently lazy, going back to doing the small things was the only option. It happened exactly as the old adage says, giving what you most wish to receive is the best way to receive it. The shift from grand gestures to daily small acts of kindness began and it created a network effect of tiny, everyday acts that offered immense fulfillment.

With the summation of dozens of tiny gestures of love, it became a new language that allowed us to communicate our love and experience the grand-gesture-like feelings. Gottlieb reminds us that marriage isn't a passion-fest; it's more like a partnership formed to run a very small, mundane, and often boring nonprofit business. Making the conscious choice to love in the tiny ways that present themselves every day has given me more joy and fulfillment than hundreds of grand gestures combined.

114

Becoming is better than being.

—Carol Dweck,
Mindset

There is really only one difference between a fixed mindset and a growth mindset, and that is choice. When we choose to see challenges as exciting instead of threatening, we actively choose to see them as opportunities for growth. We've all felt the world is out to get us or that we're simply not built for the adversities life throws our way. Or, as in my case, that we're not built to succeed the way our peers are.

I was always aware, growing up, of what I lacked. Whether it was being short, unathletic, or not talented in music like my siblings, I avoided circumstances that would place me in that position whenever possible. In the things I professed myself inadequate for, I never once considered I might one day attain that skill, nor what other skills I might possess instead. I lived the first half of my life etching my trajectory in stone based on the shortcomings of my own comparison to others.

A fixed mindset is a victim mentality, a get-out-of-jail-free card that gives our excuses strength. I never thought I was smart growing up, so I would actively play the part of a subpar student whenever a school challenge arose. People don't realize it, but bad grades require effort. You must actively choose to give incorrect responses and

227

actively choose to invest less effort, because at the very least, you'll be consistent with who you believe yourself to be. In my first semester at college, I received straight As. Surprisingly, it was on my own initiative. I was in a new environment where no one knew me as the dumb kid, so I could choose to present a different image of myself.

Dweck explores the underlying beliefs people have about learning and intelligence. A student who believes he or she can become more intelligent understands that effort is what makes him or her stronger. As a result, that student devotes more time and effort to their studies, and this leads to higher achievements. For me, such a process was easier said than done. I often felt like an imposter, and still do today.

It's at that moment when I'm reminded that this is what growth feels like. It's uncomfortable, scary, and brings me feelings of anxiety and self-consciousness.

There are two components to the concept of a growth mindset. One is applying effort to the actual challenge in front of you. The other is having the self-belief that you're actually capable of doing so.

When you surround yourself with people who believe in you, you're more likely to achieve things you've never done before or to move toward a new version of yourself. For years, I relied on others' beliefs long before I was able to see them for myself, due to my fixed mindset. Choosing to see challenges as opportunities may not be an easy task, but I've made enough mistakes in my life to know that indulging in my own shortcomings is also a choice.

115

Never lie, never cheat, never steal.

—John Wooden,
basketball coach

I, for one, have found enormous success doing each of these things—lying, cheating, and stealing—in my life. Certainly not my proudest moments. But this trifecta of shallow character guided most of my childhood. Because I lived in a culture that eschewed lying, I was able to leverage the good trust of those around me to take what I said as sincere. It was easy for me to get away with selfish childish goals, such as getting candy, watching TV, or avoiding chores. Cheating then followed. What was the difference between lying to get what I wanted and simply deceiving the teacher to get a good grade?

I leveraged my likeability to get answers from my friends and used James Bond–style tactics, such as printing things out in a two-point font so I could read them inside my clear ballpoint pen, to obtain the answers to a test.

In the end, these behaviors led to theft. Why not steal? If these new tools could help me better navigate these difficulties, things were mine to take. I would steal things from grocery stores, from my brother and sister, and, embarrassingly, from my parents as well.

You may get away with it, which is the sinister part of this. Nobody tells you what happens to you on the inside when you do these things. John Wooden is known

Lessons to Inspire

for saying you should be more concerned with your character than your reputation, because your character is what you really are, while your reputation is merely what others think you are. The reputation I had was that I was honest, had integrity, and would never steal. In the mirror every morning, I saw my character peering back at me. I knew my good fortune, my grades, and even my parents' good graces were not earned.

This experience is similar to receiving a first-place trophy and getting a parade, but being numb to the experience. It's like eating your favorite dish without tasting it. As an adult, I do my best daily to be mindful of my past relationship with these vices. Just as some people are addicted to drugs or abusive relationships, I know I could quickly make things easier in my life if I were to regress, but there's no value in that. With two children who watch my every move, and a wife who knows I'm capable of better, it's a constant reminder to do the right thing and it can be hard.

Until recently, I didn't realize how difficult it can be to make progress in life if you follow strong values and integrity. My victories are not as frequent as they once were. Being able to look myself in the mirror every morning and not feel ashamed, but proudly earning my results, even if I get in trouble, even if I come in last place, even if I'm financially unstable, offers a feeling of fulfillment that getting zapped to the finish line could never offer.

230

116

People look at you strangely, say you changed.
Like you worked that hard to stay the same.

—Jay-Z,
rapper, entrepreneur

Growing up known as a funny kid during grade school and high school, I not only identified with my persona, I was positive this was the only version of myself. Moreover, it was reinforced by family and friends, who affirmed the notion that I should act a certain way. After nearly a decade in the professional workforce, this idea of myself began to cause conflict. There was no need for me to be the funny one anymore. I didn't want to be the creative one anymore; I wanted to be the one people took seriously.

It was not well received when I began to change and act differently. When I did, I would receive laughs, but not the type I had become accustomed to.

Deciding to be different required a change of mindset. I had to unlearn previous behaviors and adopt new ways of thinking and being. It was hard. My only praise or affirmation came from myself. I told myself that who I was becoming was someone going in the right direction. I was always told who I was, and decoupling from that reinforced identity was frightening. Who was I to want more? Who was I to want to change who I was? I was also secretly looking for clues that would force me to believe change was a bad idea, even though I wanted it. I had a fixed mindset, where I was either good at it or not. Failure was the affirmation of my limited abilities to change.

I remember going out once, years after I had seen the same people who knew me as the funny one, only for them to see a newer version of myself that was more serious, analytic, and also athletic. They told me they didn't like this version of me. Not only was I saddened, it also brought me back to the very moment when I began this journey, wondering if it was all an act. I've come to realize that who people know us as is merely who we have decided to present to them, over and over. Even when they're close to me, I embrace the daily hard work it takes to not only become the person I want to be, but to never regress to who I was or thought myself to be.

Understandably, people want to have a version of you that better serves them, but equally, it is up to you to decide whether that version is the one that best serves you.

117

Always be prepared to start.

—Joe Montana,
pro football player

As the saying goes, luck is when preparation meets opportunity. For years, I wondered why this was so. I'd have minimal opportunities coming my way, but I'd simply wait for the world to give me amazing things. In failing to manifest, never visualizing my dream, never striving to make it a reality, I spent many years of my career being unable to experience the things I could have. Once, I received career advice that suggested I act and do things as I would if I held the position I was hoping to one day hold.

During the days when I was motivated, I played a character who was more eager, mindful, and disciplined than I really was, but on days when I was not motivated, I would revert to an even lesser version of myself. It took a good look in the mirror to realize laziness was the reason for my lack of consistency.

I know it's hard to prepare every day for the mere possibility that opportunities may present themselves, but I've also seen what not doing anything gets you. At the time, I didn't yet have evidence that sacrificing today would bear fruit tomorrow. I've come to realize that the only thing I can count on is that without work today, there surely won't be fruit tomorrow. There's no value in being unprepared for upcoming opportunities.

It took being nearly fifteen years in my industry before I was asked to provide consulting services. The skills I'd acquired over the years, which at the time seemed worthless, became my edge as my business grew. The majority of my consulting business is the execution of various tasks that I once considered menial, but they now attract clients willing to pay thousands of dollars for them.

It was only through an investment in the unknown, gaining skills for the opportunity in front of me, that I'm able to provide the value that I do today. Joe Montana was convinced that winners envision their dreams first. They want them with all their hearts, and they expect them to become reality. I have not only found this to be true, but also that I need to be willing to bet everything on the opportunities I want to have in my life in order to be presented with them. It's possible it may never come to pass, but one thing is certain: if you do not spend time today preparing for tomorrow's opportunity, you will sadly start believing in luck.

118

Faith and fear both demand you believe in something you cannot see.

—Bob Proctor,
Canadian writer

When I started my consultancy, every day would begin a bit differently. Some days I was very much in control and stood confidently, looking at the intense, pressure-filled days laid out for me. Other days, I'd sit in my office chair, paralyzed by the tasks at hand. My meditations and attempts to calm my mind always came down to two things: faith and fear. When I was confident of my abilities, I could attack each day without mercy, actively making decisions and advocating for the direction and guidance I would provide to these multi-million-dollar companies. Then there were (and still are today) the days when the fear of failure and my lack of faith in my own abilities makes me see my actions through a lens that forces me to question everything.

What if my recommendation is not a good idea? What if I lack the necessary experience to be able to sit at this table? What if I'm merely an imposter who obtained his position by fraud? Faith and fear have a unique relationship; they are symbiotic rather than mutually exclusive. I would often try to fully eradicate one so the other could have room to flourish, but this was an impossibility. It wasn't until I was completely defeated in this pursuit that I actually began to harness the power of these two conflicting ways of being.

They say the greatest mistake you can make in life is to be continually fearing you will make one. In accepting that I will always to some degree be fearful of failure, but that I will always have faith that I can succeed, I began to see the necessity of both ways of being. In order to overcome fear, I must have faith, and faith takes me just far enough so that fear returns.

You can use this never-ending cycle to your advantage by simply knowing one always precedes the other. You don't need to clear the fear and anxiety that clutter up the path of your goals in life; you simply need to continue forward regardless. As Bob Proctor explains, faith is the ability to see the invisible and believe in the impossible. It is what enables believers to receive what the masses think is impossible. I've come to accept the fact that failure is a probability, while success is always possible. I just need to know which part of the cycle I'm in.

119

There is not they lived happily ever after, it's more they worked happily ever after.

—Carol Dweck,
Mindset

I don't know why, but when I first heard this, it felt like a huge burden was lifted from my shoulders. I used to believe love would magically pull you and your spouse into the future. The only thing you had to do was sit back and enjoy the ride.

I began to take the foot off the gas almost immediately after getting married. Having earned my wife's good graces already, I believed it was my turn to coast. I had proved my worth by putting in the time. I cringe at this mindset today, not only because it was lazy, but also because it was self-centered.

I've come to learn that marriage is a choice. Staying in love is a daily choice. Continuously finding ways to innovate and iterate your love in order to keep it fresh and alive is a daily choice, though it is easier said than done. Many times I asked myself, what's the point? Why strive for even more happiness if she's already happy?

In the beginning of a relationship, you'll do anything to show your love. You look for every opportunity to show your affection and care. All of this lead to the major milestones of a relationship, such as moving in together, getting married, buying a house, and having children. Happily ever after is merely a moment in time. If you want more of those, you must work to achieve it. This was something that struck me as completely exhausting.

My first thought was that love should not be considered work. But where else in your life do you put forth zero effort and gain everything in return? From personal experience, I know what a relationship looks like when you stop watering it and giving it sunlight. Rather than simply dying, it grows weeds. At some point you need to truly ask yourself, is this other person's life that much of a priority to me? If it is, what are you willing to do today to truly make your relationship better? Moreover, it is not only about chores and gifts. It's also about finding the small moments every day that help nourish, grow, and inspire your spouse on their journey to becoming their best selves. In my eyes, this is more than just the title of a husband; it carries meaning and purpose.

In the mornings, I have every reason to work as hard as I do for my family as I do for my career, because working toward happily ever after offers an unrivaled sense of fulfillment. I can't imagine many other things in this life that are as gratifying as being of service to those you love, knowing that your actions, no matter how small, make their lives better on a daily basis. The best part of a marriage is its reciprocity and symbiotic nature. I never have to ask her to do the same. This is a way by which anyone can find happily ever after, simply by working toward it one moment at a time.

120

I'm always doing what I cannot do yet.
In order to learn how to do it.

—Vincent van Gogh,
French painter

When I first started my career, I began in catering, which led to restaurants, which led to management, which ultimately led to me working in corporate food service. Having arrived there, I thought I would do it for the rest of my life. As a twenty-six-year-old, I managed multi-million-dollar accounts for Fortune 500 companies. I remember watching my counterparts jump to attention for someone their exact age who had taken a different path. Someone who was an executive. There was something different about them; they seemed confident, articulate, and even the fabric of their clothes seemed luxurious.

Though I aspired to be a chef, this is what I found to be my true calling. Fortunately, I was surrounded by executives at the account I managed, because the account's office was located across the street from our corporate headquarters. As a result, my COO would frequently attend my meetings with the CEO and other executives or investors. Because I ran a fairly tight ship, I was often praised in front of the client for the efficiency and profitability of our operations.

Then they requested I meet with my counterparts. They would suggest tactics and strategies so their account could become as productive and profitable as mine. I excelled at this and one day was asked to become a regional manager, but I was terrified and felt like I had conned my way there. Was I really good enough? Or did I simply have an amazing staff?

This is where the quote really came in handy. I learned you should say yes when you are up for a promotion. You can figure out how to do it later. I've been a regional manager, director, and national account manager during the course of my career, each time believing my current skill set would impede my success. My experience has been that leadership often does not care about your skill set. What really matters is that you're willing to hold yourself accountable for completing the task. In this role, you become their problem solver, and executives are constantly dealing with problems.

There's something special that happens when you put yourself in a no-way-out situation. When your only option is to succeed, you tend to do just that. Furthermore, you may surprise yourself with how well you adapt. You may often see your best efforts as the new norm now. It's that simple.

Almost a decade later, I'm an executive with the exact same fears and anxieties I had before, but I now know that attempting something I can't yet do doesn't mean I'm a fraud or imposter. Rather, it means I'm taking a first step toward learning and growing new skills, which would otherwise have remained dormant if not for these exact circumstances.

121

*Courage is what it takes to stand up and speak;
courage is also what it takes to sit down and
listen.*

—Richard Branson,
entrepreneur, founder of the Virgin Group

Be the last to speak. This is one of the most
valuable lessons I've ever learned. Leaders don't
sway others into agreeing with their ideas immediately.
They allow others to speak first and be heard, before
voicing their own views. It sounds easy, but I've rarely, if
ever, put this advice into practice. To take advantage of
an opportunity, I always had to speak my mind. Having
spent most of my life being the first to speak, I believe this
has prevented my peers from experiencing growth dozens
if not hundreds of times. I'm not saying I'm responsible
for their actions, but I'm definitely responsible for creating
an environment and posturing that my opinions are the
more valuable.

Often, I asserted I had a solution, an idea, an
innovative approach. For the sole purpose of being in
the spotlight, regardless of how this impacted everything
else, I would specifically sway the group around me and
charm them into agreeing with my point of view, not
for any particular reason other than to be the one in the
spotlight.

As long as my opinion was validated, I didn't care
about anything else. Not only did speaking first make
me feel smarter, it made me feel superior as well. If I

were ever last, I would not only be less than, I would be worthless.

Often, this resulted in ripples that affected others, and even my business. My personal life suffered from this for years. I spoke without listening. Being denied the spotlight, or worse, giving it to someone who obviously won't enjoy it as much, was a missed opportunity for someone who craves attention. In turn, this fueled my ego's growth and accelerated the growth of blind arrogance. When I pass up the opportunity to speak, I felt anxious, and my skin would crawl. I'd ask myself, why bother listening to others, what can they possibly offer that I already don't know? After almost thirty-five years of speaking first and not listening to others, my progress slowed everywhere in my life. My relationships with friends, family, and career all reached critical points. They had become one-sided.

At some point, any insight or advantages I held were outdated. They were no longer beneficial to anyone, including myself. It was this calcified way of thinking that showed me just how harmful this behavior was to myself and those around me. At this point, listening became the only remedy. This helped me realize how valuable other people's opinions are. By accepting that anyone could teach me something of value, I was able to let go of my own inferiority complex. Learning from others is the key to sustained growth in life if you're brave enough to simply sit down, listen, and realize that, sometimes, not speaking is the most valuable thing you can offer.

122

*You can't tell big dreams
to small-minded people.*

—Steve Harvey,
actor, comedian

Most of the things I've done in my life were based on what I thought others believed I should do. From a young age, I followed what my parents said, acted like my siblings, and behaved like my friends. In this way, a culture of acceptance was fostered that assumes that acting or being in a particular manner helps validate who you are. Provided you follow a certain path, all will be well and good.

It occurs to all of us at some point in our lives that when we begin to question whether what we're doing is what we really want to do, or it is merely what we've been conditioned to do. The moment is not an easy one. It's when you realize you have to divert from what you know and change how you are perceived by those closest to you in order to fulfill your own hopes and dreams.

At one time, I thought people were wrong when they tried to get you to stay in your lane. I see it now as a way of protecting yourself, making sure you aren't hurt by doing something you haven't announced as your capability. Taking the risk of breaking the mold isn't enough; you must be willing to accept their perspective when you realize they were right. Failing, coming home with your tail between your legs, is actually okay, because the very act of taking risks begins to develop the muscles you need to try something new in the future. When I've attempted something, people may have been right when I failed. In those cases where I've achieved something, people have been wrong. The trick is to not become resentful of other people's opinions and beliefs about your capabilities, but to use that very moment of pushback as a sign that you're onto something. It's a moment when signals change.

The reason people want to pull others back is that each of us plays an integral role in each other's lives. When someone does something outside of the norm, it has more to do with him or her than it does with you. Change affects their ecosystem. If they're not open to it, it becomes a threat to their world and, ultimately, who they are. Don't assume others will support your goals; rather, accept that achieving something new in life represents change for you, and you may not fully believe you are capable.

You can't tell big dreams to small-minded people. Not because they won't believe in or support you, but because they're not responsible for championing your ambitions. Only you are. It is okay, though, because whatever it is you wish to accomplish in life is yours alone. Don't allow others to get in your way, because your dream was never given to them and is never theirs to take away.

123

Don't ever feel bad for making a decision about your own life that upsets other people.

—Isaiah Hankel,
writer, scientist

Growing up in conformity is easy. As children we tend to gravitate toward what is socially acceptable in our community. My very identity was formed in this way. My abundance and confidence increased as I became more socially accepted. Considering my entire community was behind me, I assumed I'd always receive the same advocacy and validation toward my goals and dreams. I based my self-confidence in facing the world's challenges on the external validation provided by my community.

The problem here was that I mistook their acceptance for support. It was when I began making decisions outside of this framework that I began to feel the effects of this flawed approach to life. My odd career choice, plus getting engaged at the age of twenty-four, both seemed to rub some people the wrong way. I would actually apologize for my actions and how they made others feel, trying desperately to get back into their good graces.

External validation is an addiction, an easy thing to return to, but once the dopamine was released, I would feel not only disappointed in myself, but also a lack of identity. It begged the question, who am I if my actions are being questioned by the same group that gave me so much confidence in the first place? How could I stray from the path? It was only right that I abide by the community's expectations, so why am I compelled to try something I deeply desire?

Isaiah Hankel says we are not responsible for the happiness of others. We are responsible for our own happiness. It was sad to think I would feel ashamed and even guilty when I was doing things that fulfilled me.

When I stopped trying so hard to gain acceptance from the very community that birthed my confidence, everything began to turn around. Making decisions that others won't agree with is an eventuality. Oftentimes it's those closest to you who are the first with that disbelief, but how you deal with it in that exact moment can be the difference between the life you have today and the life of your dreams. Faced with beliefs that clash, and deciding to bet on yourself, it's a tough moment. However, a far more painful experience is putting someone else's opinion or thoughts above your own. Before, I would get angry at those around me if my decisions upset them. Now I get angry only if I abandon my own hopes and dreams in exchange for social acceptance.

124

*Focusing your life solely on making a buck
shows a certain poverty of ambition.*

—Barack Obama,
44th president of the United States

During the year I'm writing this, I will have
surpassed $450,000 in earnings. It wasn't until
the end of the year that this quote Barack Obama shared
became so important to me. Having made $200,000 then
$300,000, and so on, I was confident my life would become
increasingly happier as I made more money. Money has
done only one thing for me. That was to make my life
slightly more convenient when dealing with financial
issues. That's it. It hasn't made me a better person, and a
part of me wishes I had never made this much, because
of what it did to skew my perception of value.

Having purchased expensive things such as new cars,
clothes, or the latest technology, I came to realize that one
day I'd be ashamed to show off that part of myself. My
embarrassment increased as I made it clear that I would
use it exclusively for material purposes. When you use
your money on yourself, it can feel like being the only
person on a large life raft, watching others drown outside
a sinking vessel. There's a fine line between wealth
being a bridge that leads to empty career success and
fading treasures or a bridge that enables you to provide
tremendous value to the people you care about.

At the end of this year, the most meaningful things I could recall doing were when I spent my money on unique experiences and travel with my wife and kids, a getaway holiday to spend time with my sister, a dinner with my brother at a restaurant of his choosing, a weekend in a luxury hotel with my parents, or boarding my dog in a private suite. It wasn't the cost of these experiences that was the value, but spending my money on those I love and cared for was extremely fulfilling, whereas pouring the money I made into material things did absolutely nothing for me. This taught me that each of these experiences could also have been done with the money I made five years ago. I might not have been able to purchase the same level of experience, but living with lack prevented me from believing that fulfilling experiences were even an option for me.

Only when you attach your wagon to something larger than yourself can you realize your true potential. We think not having enough money is the barrier to what we want in life, but making enough money and actually getting those things can become the new barrier. It makes us blind to the things that really matter. I used to drive a Honda Civic filled with friends. When I drove my Porsche, I always seemed to be alone.

125

Nothing worth having comes easy.

—Theodore Roosevelt,
26th president of the United States

After nearly five years on this journey, I can tell you that doing hard things sucks. It is draining, it deflates, and on many occasions it makes me depressed. The ability to do hard things seems to have been a talent given to everyone but me. My behavior in times of difficulty was to avoid difficult endeavors. There seemed to be no value in making myself uncomfortable.

I had never experienced what a life would be like when I actually overcome obstacles. I lived the majority of my life as if I were on a battlefield, and everyone around me was experiencing hardship, getting wounded or killed. I've always been able to achieve what I desired in life with minimal difficulty, so why bother? Without experiencing difficult situations in life, I didn't know I was slowly atrophying the muscles necessary to adapt to the challenges of the future.

There is a saying that ease is a greater threat to progress than hardship, and this is absolutely true. The difficult aspects of my life began to present themselves when I was approaching my mid-thirties. Experiencing the death of loved ones, maintaining a marriage, an economic downturn, the challenges of being a parent, weakening friendships, and career stagnation, I was ill-equipped to cope. I simply didn't think it was possible to do something despite how I felt. I look back with humility after having experienced hardships and would say that, regardless of getting on the other side, my struggles were most likely not even a fraction of what most people experience throughout their lives.

The most valuable lesson I learned was that avoiding difficult things in life not only makes you vulnerable to failure in the future, it also ensures you live your life merely as an existence. Being confronted with difficulty and actively seeking difficulty produce a perspective that allows you to fully appreciate your journey. You'll see every challenge presented to you through a lens of opportunity and growth.

According to David Goggins, when you feel you've reached your absolute limit, you're actually only at 40 percent of your capacity; if you can push through the difficulty, you'll find your best self.

Knowing you're able to sit through and choose a challenging path is an indescribable confidence booster. After finally turning the corner, you realize you're on the verge of reaching the finish line, experiencing the moment before the moment will always affirm that facing challenges always leads to fulfillment and arguably some of the most satisfying instances in life.

Bibliography

Books read in preparation for this book:

12 Rules for Life, Jordan B. Peterson
12 Week Year, Brian P. Moran and Michael Lennington
13 Things That Mentally Strong People Don't Do, Amy Morin
15 Commitments of Conscious Leadership, Jim Dethmer,
   Diana Chapman, Kaley Warner Klemp
365 Dalai Lama: Daily Advice from the Heart, Dalai Lama XIV
48 Laws of Power, Robert Greene
4-Hour Work Week, Timothy Ferriss
The 5 A.M. Club, Robin Sharma
5 Second Rule, Mel Robbins
59 Seconds, Richard Wiseman
The Alchemist, Paulo Coelho
The Algebra of Happiness, Scott Galloway
All You Have to Do Is Ask, Wayne Baker
Answers Unleashed, Olympia LePoint
The Art of Logic, Eugenia Cheng
The Art of Public Speaking, Dale Carnegie
Art of Racing in the Rain, Garth Stein
The Art of Seduction, Robert Greene
As a Man Thinketh, James Allen

Atomic Habits, James Clear

Attached: Are you Anxious, Avoidant or Secure?, Amir Levine, and Rachel S. F. Heller

Awaken the Giant Within, Tony Robbins

Be Fearless: 5 Principles for a Life of Breakthroughs and Purpose, Jean Case

Becoming, Michelle Obama

Best Job Ever!, C. K. Bray

Beyond Good and Evil, Friedrich Nietzsche

Beyond Order, Jordan B. Peterson

The Book of Joy, 14th Dalai Lama, Desmond Tutu, and Douglas Abrams

The Buddha and the Badass, Vishen Lakhiani

Can't Hurt Me, David Goggins

Captivate, Vanessa Van Edwards

The Charge, Brendon Burchard

The Charisma Myth, Olivia Fox Cabane

The Coffeehouse Investor, John J. Boyle

Compound Effect, Darren Hardy

Conscious, Annaka Harris

Content Rules, Ann Handley and C. C. Chapman

The Courage Habit, Kate Swoboda

The Daily Stoic, Ryan Holiday and Stephen Hanselman

Dare to Lead, Brené Brown

The Decision, Kevin Hart

Digital Minimalism, Cal Newport

The Discomfort Zone, Farrah Storr

Do Breathe, Michael Townsend Williams

Elevate, Robert Glazer

The End of Marketing, Carlos Gil

Epic Content Marketing, Joe Pulizzi

The Execution Factor, Kim Perell

Extreme Ownership, Jocko Willink and Leif Babin

Facebook Marketing, Justin R. Levy

Fast Feast Repeat, Gin Stephens

Bibliography

The Fifth Agreement, Don Miguel Ruiz, Don Jose Ruiz, and Janet Mills

Find Your Why, Simon Sinek

First Things First, Stephen R. Covey, A. Roger Merrill, and Rebecca R. Merrill

Flaming Hot, Richard Montanez

For Small Creatures Such as We, Sasha Sagan

The Four Agreements, Don Miguel Ruiz

F*ck Content Marketing, Randy Frisch

The Gifts of Imperfection, Brené Brown

Greenlights, Matthew McConaughey

Grit, Angela Duckworth

A Handbook for New Stoics, Massimo Pigliucci and Gregory Lopez

Happiness Equation, Neil Pasricha

High Performance Habits, Brendon Burchard

How to Be a Bawse, Lilly Singh

How to Be a Stoic, Massimo Pigliucci

Hustle Harder, Curtis "50 Cent" Jackson

I Can't Make This Up, Kevin Hart and Neil Strauss

The Ideal Team Player, Patrick Lencioni

The IT Marketing Crash Course, Susan C. Baier

Jab, Jab, Jab, Right Hook, Gary Vaynerchuk

Kitchen Confidential, Anthony Bourdain

The Laws of Human Nature, Robert Greene

The Leading Brain, Friederike Fabritius and Hans W. Hagemann

Life Lessons, Elisabeth Kübler-Ross and David Kessler

Living Forward, Michael Hyatt and Daniel Harkavy

Long Walk to Freedom, Nelson Mandela

Loserthink, Scott Adams

The Lucifer Effect, Philip Zimbardo

The Magna Carta of Exponentiality, Vusi Thembekwayo

Mastery, Robert Greene

Mindset, Carol S. Dweck

The Miracle Morning, Hal Elrod

Money: Master the Game, Tony Robbins

The Myth of Sanity, Martha Stout
Nine Lies about Work, Marcus Buckingham and Ashley Goodall
No Excuses, Brian Tracy
No More Mr. Nice Guy, Robert A. Glover
Perfectly Yourself, Matthew Kelly
Permission Marketing, Seth Godin
The Power of Bad, John Tierney and Roy F. Baumeister
The Power of No, James Altucher and Claudia Azula Altucher
The Power of Vulnerability, Brené Brown
The Practicing Mind, Thomas M. Sterner
Presence, Amy Cuddy
The Probability of Miracles, Wendy Wunder
Procrastination on Purpose, Rory Vaden
Psycho Cybernetics, Maxwell Maltz
Quiet, Susan Cain
Reinvent Yourself, James Altucher
The Revenue Growth Habit, Alex Goldfayn
The Ride of a Lifetime, Robert Iger
Ruthless Elimination of Hurry, John Mark Comer
Sapiens, Yuval Noah Harari
The Science of Intelligent Achievement, Isaiah Hankel
The Science of Money, Brian Tracy
The Second Mountain, David Brooks
See You at the Top, Zig Ziglar
See You on the Internet, Avery Swartz
Seven Habits of Highly Effectful People, Stephen R. Covey
Stick with It, Sean D. Young
Stillness Is the Key, Ryan Holiday
Strength in Stillness, Bob Roth
The Subtle Art of Not Giving a F*ck, Mark Manson
The Sunflower, Simon Wiesenthal
Surrounded by Idiots, Thomas Erikson
Talking to Strangers, Malcolm Gladwell
TED Talks, Chris Anderson

Bibliography

Think and Grow Rich, Napoleon Hill
Think Like a Monk, Jay Shetty
Think Small, Owain Service and Rory Gallagher
Time and How You Spend It, James Wallman
Tribe of Mentors, Timothy Ferriss
The Trusted Advisor, David H. Maister, Charles H. Green, and
  Robert M. Galford
Two Awesome Hours, Josh Davis
Ultralearning, Scott H. Young
Unfu*k Yourself, Gary John Bishop
Unlimited Power, Tony Robbins
Unshakeable, Tony Robbins
The Untethered Soul, Michael A. Singer
The Upside of Your Dark Side, Todd Kashdan and Robert Biswas-
  Diener
Walden, Henry David Thoreau
We're All Marketers, Nico De Bruyn
When Breath Becomes Air, Paul Kalanithi
Who Moved My Cheese, Spencer Johnson
Who Will Cry When You Die, Robin Sharma
Will, Will Smith and Mark Manson
You're Not Listening, Kate Murphy
Your Life or Your Money, Vicki Robin and Joe Dominguez

About the Author

 **Gary Batara** is Vice President of Marketing at a Y-Combinator Top 100 hyper growth startup in the San Francisco Bay Area. Batara earned his bachelor's degree in business administration and his MBA from the University of Phoenix. In his studies, he had a specialized focus on marketing. Achieving distinction, he earned membership in the Delta Mu Delta International Academic Honor Society and the National Society of Leadership and Success. With a career spanning fifteen years, Batara has gained extensive expertise in marketing, hosting a notable trajectory that includes roles at prominent Fortune 500 companies as Google, ISS Global, Baseline Ventures, as well as PowerPlant and Astanor Capital-backed startups. His contributions have been pivotal in propelling companies toward hypergrowth, surpassing revenue milestones that exceed the billion-dollar mark.

Batara lives in the San Francisco Bay Area with his wife Marilyn and enjoys spending quality time with their two children, Dylan and Jake. They enjoy vacationing in Hawaii and indulging in their passion for movies. In his spare time, Batara enjoys competitive weightlifting.

Gary Batara may be reached by e-mail at: **garybatara72@gmail.com.**